IN PRAISE

When the Berlin wall was taken down and both sides were exposed and free, it took a lot of courage and braun to accomplish such a thing. It was believed it was worth the risk. When a person is willing to take down their own walls and expose themselves in order to have freedom of the heart, mind and soul, that takes even more courage and an enormous inner strength. For Alan, it too was worth the risk.

Anyone willing to do such a thing and then to put it out there for the world to see, some to judge and many to learn from, it is worth taking the time to explore such a revelation. This book should be read with an open heart and mind and a willingness to take the risk and the journey that Alan took to have his inner freedom and quite possibly your own!

Sheina Jacobson

"Is there anyone of us who can honestly say we have not had to work through our "ego" issues? Thinking we "know it all" and waking up to the shocking realization that it's all made up, Alan Freedman shows us how humility and vulnerability, combined with finding God, brings us back to the truth...that Love is all there is."

Lori S. Rubenstein JD,
Author of
Forgiveness: Heal Your Past and Find the Peace You Deserve

The Walk by Alan Freedman is an unveiling of heart and soul from someone who has been through transformation. Alan has experienced "religion" in two different expressions, that both ended up in ritual and routine. He is now an advocate of relationships.

Early in the book, Alan met God in a new depth, through Alan's failure as a husband. He came to realize that being a "celebrity" Christian was empty and without purpose. God showed Alan his own heart and began setting Alan free when he began to love his bride like Christ loves the Church.

Alan's story echoes with many of us. It is a good thing, God did not show him too far into the future, or Alan may have turned away in fear and not found fulfillment.

The Walk is to be read like a thoughtful stroll, not a sprint. It will challenge you and if you let it...change you.

**Lee Balinas. - M. Div.,
Ordained Baptist Minister**

While reading through these chapters, several things stuck out in my mind. The first being - it wouldn't have mattered to me whether (we) the writer and I were the same race, religion, sex, or frankly from the same planet. The fact that he makes himself so transparent and allows his own vulnerability to be laid bare, makes the invitation "come walk with me" an easy YES!

I am looking forward to the challenge of walking with the rabbi and seeking ways to grow myself and serve Creator and Creation in the paragon of the greatest shepherd that ever was, is and is to come - Yeshua HaMashiach! A & Ω

Thanks for enriching my life and showing the way to be a servant! And most of all - thanks for walking with me!!

Jacquie Pounden

The Walk®

Discover your life purpose by

exercising the courage to question – everything!

Written by

Alan E. Freedman

Your Personal Tour Guide

Copyright© 2012 – Alan E. Freedman

The Walk®

www.WalkBook.com

LOC: 2012921874

ISBN (978-1481027113) Paperback

Publishing by

Bootstrap Publishing - **BootstrapPublishing.com**

DM BookPro – **DMBookPro.com**

DEDICATION

This book is dedicated to all the people who aspire and commit to reaching their zenith and personal summit, and thereby, possess the courage to question and challenge *everything* that they and the status quo, hold to be true. These are the people that are changing themselves inside out and by extension, our world. These are the difference makers.

I salute you.

CONTENTS

PREFACE

The book you are holding in your hands, The Walk®, has not been put there by random accident. It is by perfect DIVINE design. You see, this book was written exclusively for *you*. Even now, you feel its draw – don't you?

"What is my life's purpose," you have been asking yourself. "Why am I here?" You are about to discover those answers – but it will require a personal reset – a starting over. Ready?

The Walk® begins with the understanding that if you are to succeed in attaining your personal highest and best, you must first know what destination you are heading for: Your Life Purpose. There will surely be obstacles along the route. It will be essential to identify them in advance so you can devise effective strategies to navigate around them when they appear. One crucially important tactic that you will want to employ (much sooner than later) will be the one of holding the joy you will experience as you make progress solidly in your mind and heart. Do not let go of it!

You will need to recruit a gifted team and crew for the journey, for no one can do this successfully alone. I will give you counsel which will empower you to choose wisely and will instill life-giving confidence. One of your greatest adversaries will be relying on what you think you already know! Your illusion of knowledge can easily fool you. You will be required to get out of your own way. I will help you in this crucially important area.

What force could have changed a person who, at one time was a sworn enemy of the gay/lesbian community and convinced that they were a scourge upon the earth? This person believed this community to be a blight upon all that was Holy; they were a people condemned to eternal darkness. What unseen power was it that changed this person to one who is now a deeply committed advocate, and a person proudly proclaiming a message of equality and a level playing field for all? Why are the biblical scriptures that are used to renounce same-sex equality inadmissible in the court of intellectual honesty?

Would you have been willing to wager a bet, as to which political convention GOD would have shown up at earlier this year? Would HE manifest HIMSELF as a donkey or an elephant? Just where does the DIVINE throw HIS heavenly support? Perhaps that depends on whom you are talking about. The GOD of Abraham, Isaac and Jacob? Or the "god" that has been reduced to an automobile bumper sticker and made in the image of its driver. Do our political leaders have any idea whatsoever as to divine decree, or are HIS standards too socialist?

Many talk passionately of the need for the United States to return to the culture of authentic capitalism the country once knew. Did the United States practice capitalism in the purest form – ever? Just what did the authors of original capitalism envision? What form of capitalism should we be embracing going forward so that *all* have an equal opportunity to experience their highest and best and *all* benefit greatly because of it? A capitalism of the heart. This type of doctrine is sincerely "Of the people, by the people, and for the people. Would Adam Smith, the father of capitalism and economics, be viewed as a leftist today?"

Virtually every significant and positive world-changing personality throughout history has been branded a revolutionary. They each stood proudly yet humbly in the face of the status quo and said "No more." These people were the ones who not only saw and comprehended injustice, inequality, cruelty, and victimization, but also placed their personal reputations, public standings and their very lives firmly on the line and demanded change - because it was the right thing to do. They were the agents of true transformation. We are desperately in global need of more people just like them - today!

This is a book about exercising the courage to question what you have believed to be true regarding some of the most hotly debated, emotionally charged and divisive issues of our times. By taking these challenges, you will be able to discover your own personal life purpose and experience an eternal life-changing point in your life journey. You will then be able to give a voice toward effective and powerful change in a world that desperately needs DIVINE heart surgery. We are so desperately in need of a global reset.

✡ ✡ ✡

ACKNOWLEDGEMENTS

No meaningful creation of any nature can be accomplished alone; this book is no different.

I have been so very blessed throughout my life, to have had such gifted people come across my path, in abundant numbers. All of them have played a role in *my personal walk.* I would like to single out some of the more notable ones.

Thank you to my mother, Grace, who gave me life and from whom I inherited her love for GOD's animal creations; Wayne Sproule, my earliest spiritual mentor, who selflessly gave of his time and his heart; my intern, Cindy Crossett, who reminds me regularly of the importance of walking my talk. Thank you to all of the followers of **The Walk®,** who faithfully stood with me while this work was evolving and who, by doing so, provided the motivation to keep me going; my editor, Annie Berardini-Rivers, who graciously put up with the initial work of a budding author who, when it came to the technical side of preparing a manuscript for publishing, didn't know what he didn't know. I can never adequately repay my dear friend Lynne Palmer Janelle, who faithfully read what I thought was a finished manuscript and then lovingly but honestly, told me what I needed to hear.

Their caring insights resulted in **The Walk**® being a deeper and more meaningful experience for all.

Thank you to my daughter, Jennifer, who by being authentically herself provided me with the potential to eventually love a community that I, at one time had dismissed. Also, to my dear friend Jacquie, who has been an extremely important part of my "checks and balances," as I've been personally evolving. To my wife Fran, who is not only my best friend, but also my greatest teacher on many levels. I am what I am today and will become tomorrow, because of you. You are my life's balance: my eyes when I don't see what I should be seeing, my ears when I don't hear what I should be hearing, my heart when I don't feel what I should be feeling, my mind when I don't understand what I should be understanding. I love you.

Last, but certainly not least, my GOD and my CREATOR. Thank you for drawing the people and the resources to me at just the right times, and for giving me the awareness, that these gifts were meant for me. I have been, and continue to be, the beneficiary of a harvest of inestimable value. With humility, I love the person you have created and continue to shape.

INTRODUCTION

*"He/she who needs to be right, is in a
prison of their own creation."*
Alan E. Freedman

If everything you now believe to be true were a lie – when would you want to know? When it comes to some of the most impassioned, hotly-debated and divisive issues of our day, when was the last time you honestly questioned yourself, as to why you believe what you believe? Have you ever? This takes great courage! However, you must question – if *you* are to discover *your* life purpose – what *you* were uniquely created for!

We live in a time, where virtually everything, ought to be questioned, challenged, and when appropriate, changed or eliminated. A spirit of greed, corruption and prideful self-righteousness, practiced by a powerful few, has taken on a life of its own, while creation picks up the "tab." The entire universe is crying out for change. We desperately need a worldwide reset.

The Walk® is both a simulated guided tour and a personal journey which provides at designated "rest stops," opportunities for quiet introspection and courageous self-questioning. Along the path, I transparently share with you my own life experiences concerning some of the most impassioned, divisive and controversial issues of our day. I reveal where I once stood, as GOD's self-appointed gatekeeper of all truth, one with all the answers, to what was behind the 180 degree turn I underwent, to where I am now, one with more questions than answers. I had been blind and didn't know it. I desperately needed DIVINE heart surgery – I got it!

What force could have changed the heart of a person, that at one time was a sworn enemy of the gay/lesbian community, convinced that they were a scourge upon the earth, a blight upon all that was Holy, a people condemned to eternal darkness, to one who is now a committed advocate, a person proudly proclaiming a message of equality and a level playing field?

Willing to wager a bet as to which political party in the United States GOD is registered with? Will he ultimately manifest HIMSELF as a donkey or an elephant? Just where does the DIVINE throw HIS heavenly support? Perhaps that depends on who you are talking about: the GOD of Abraham, Isaac and Jacob or the god that has been reduced to an automobile bumper sticker.

Many passionately talk of the need for the United States, to return to the culture of the authentic capitalism she once knew. Did she ever practice capitalism in its purest form? Just what did the authors of original capitalism envision? What form of capitalism should we be embracing going forward, so that all have an equal opportunity, to experience their highest and best, and where all benefit greatly because of it - a capitalism of the heart?

Virtually every significant and positive world-changing personality throughout history has been branded a revolutionary. They all stood proudly yet humbly in the face of the status quo, and said "no more." These were the ones who not only saw and learned of injustice, inequality and victimization, but placed personal reputation, status and life itself, firmly on the line and demanded change-because it was the right thing to do. They were the agents of change. We are desperately in global need of more people just like them-now!

I simply ask only one thing of you, as we walk together and reflect on the issues – that you choose to have a "beginner's mind," start with a clean slate, and view everything with a new heart and new eyes. It will be more than worth it! It will present you with an incredible opportunity for self-transformation!

In the end, it will always be up to you to decide what truth is – to you. You will come to know without a doubt, what your life purpose is – why you were created. This will ultimately lead to a more tolerant, forgiving, responsible and responsive planet - for all of its inhabitants.

SAMPLINGS FROM "THE WALK"®
FAITH
Back then when I knew it all.

There are words I seldom choose to use for a variety of reasons. These specific words can denote something wholly undesirable, conjure up negative attitudes, and come across as self-righteous and judgmental. These words can render me *persona non grata* as to being the beneficiary of gifts, I otherwise would have received. I can become intolerant. I can be cut off from experiencing necessary changes in my life, and a whole host of other results.

One such word is the term <u>obnoxious</u>. Look it up in the dictionary. It signifies a litany, a virtual plethora of unpleasant attributes, when associated with and imputed to a person. In Spanish, one would use words like "odioso" (the word in English means detestable) and "repugnante" (which translates as smell in English), to convey what is behind an obnoxious person. The word signifies someone seen as smelly (even if void of body odor) and detestable. This is a serious word, and should be unearthed sparingly, with great care and forethought. It bites hard and deep on its recipient.

It is with this as a backdrop, that I freely confess that I, at one time, was unequivocally and undeniably - obnoxious. I am now aware of this, because I come across people that are presently the way I once was - when I knew it all.   Just ask the people I interacted with on spiritual matters, after "I got religion." (Later on, I received the gift of faith - a big difference). When it came to matters of spirituality including correct theology, one's proper standing before GOD, living life the way the CREATOR intended for us to live it, and on and on, I had the corner on all truth. Any dissenting voices were simply followers of another gospel, who I then felt compelled to guide towards the true light, which I was holding. Was it even conceivable to imagine that they could experience a blessing greater than this? The gift I would give them. I certainly could not imagine so.

FAITH AND LIFE PARTNERS
From having all the answers, to
having more questions than answers.

It had been a number of years since I saw and heard from Carolyn. The tone in her voice and the urgency of her words left no doubt as to the extreme fragile nature of her marriage, her finances and the prognosis of her future. Like every cancer, whether an actual illness associated with a tumor or one of life's many thorns in the flesh, one may cover it up with a bandage but the festering and deterioration continue. The sources of Carolyn's many anxieties had obviously never been effectively confronted over the years. The implications of never being fully truthful with herself and her husband had now manifested themselves in myriad adverse ways. All progress begins by telling the truth.

"My husband and I do not see eye-to-eye on a whole host of important issues, and as to being in a partnership, I feel we have a team comprised of one - and I am not the one. What is at stake is my emotional well-being and sanity. I feel dishonored, disrespected, abused, like mere chattel. I need....no, WE need, to see you as soon as practical."

The bottom line was they needed to take personal responsibility for their own required changes to move forward, and not that of their partner, while choosing instead the intention of supporting and affirming the other. They needed to choose not to look at the other, as the reason for the curve balls life had thrown at them. Each needed to take personal ownership of what he or she was experiencing. They could choose to discontinue living the lives of whiners, who were focused on the problems and instead start down a path of becoming seekers of solutions. If they would both commit to seeing things anew, starting over, being openly teachable, and to not depend on what they both thought they knew, then it was not too late. Time was most certainly of the essence!

FAITH AND THE GLBT COMMUNITY
(GAY, LESBIAN, BI-SEXUAL, TRANS-GENDER)

Lorne had been involved in church ministry, as a member of a conservative evangelical denomination for years, first as a youth pastor, and eventually going to a church that was calling him to be their Senior Pastor. He was virtually without peer, when it came to possessing and applying his servant heart. When it came to carrying out what he believed was his divine calling, he was tireless. He was without compromise, when it came to faithfully proclaiming at every turn, his beloved canon. He was a master messenger and advocate, of what he truly believed to be irrefutable truth that which was beyond question, forever perfect, pure, no matter the human fallout.

His sold-out intensity of commitment, to that which he considered inviolable, sacrosanct, and unchallengeable, extended to what he believed to be GOD's final word on "the gay/lesbian issue." Simply stated, same-sex lifestyle was a choice, and a choice that had far-reaching current and eternal consequences, ending with a destiny clearly out of DIVINE favor, destined to a godless eternity. These lesser- humans, were a scourge upon HIS creation and a blight upon all that was right, moral, and GOD honoring.

One day, in a divinely inspired moment of GRACE, Lorne was visited upon, by the DIVINE heart surgeon of the universe. After his experience, he miraculously and literally, started all over again. This emotionally charged theme and his position toward it changed dramatically and opened his eyes and heart.

FAITH AND POLITICS

So there I was, in a large, predominantly socially conservative U.S. city, having dinner with a group of friends (actually, friends, as long as your political ideology lined up with theirs). A federal election was not too far in the distance. Dinner became an endless procession of gastronomical delight. The evening could not have been enhanced in any way! And then came the final course. It was preceded by a course of a different taste and flavor, a dis-course, which changed the tenor of the rest of the evening.

"Surely you will be voting for the Republican nominee?" my 'friend' inquired. I looked directly at him, as I contemplated (for what felt like hours), before giving him my reply. I was determined to both speak the truth, but also to avoid a scene and keep from tainting our relationship. When I told him my wife and I would be voting for the other guy, he literally went ballistic.

"GOD gave you a mind to use and think with, boy!" he chastised, now elevated from his seat. "That man (the candidate I had just told him I was supporting) is the anti-Christ. He is determined to bring our way of life here in America to its knees. He is pure evil. Do you not know that GOD looks down on the <u>political party name inserted here</u> and considers them anathema, accursed?"

Either my friend was privy to a degree of heretofore-unrevealed insight that clearly I was naïve to, or he was guilty of having created an emotional and intellectual prison, a self-imposed creation, keeping him from achieving his highest potential on so many levels. I chose to address the latter insight.

Chiming in, I said, "I just have to tell you, my friend: GOD is not a politician."

FAITH AND CAPITALISM

This is a hotly debated and emotionally charged theme, as well. What did the authors of capitalism have in mind? How did they envision it playing out in society? Have we gone off course, and if so, by how much? Can it be restored, or have we gone over the tipping point? Moreover, is it worth restoring, or do we need an entirely new paradigm? Do we need a form of capitalism that provides a level playing field for all, regardless of social status? Do we require a new game that rejoices, validates, and affirms, the creativity and successes of others, rather than one that does everything possible to keep people in their places? We need a capitalism "of the people, by the people and for the people." This is faith-based capitalism. Furthermore, notwithstanding the fact, that right-leaning politicians and their adherents purport a return to a capitalistic society, I doubt that many of them, and perhaps most, have even thought through what they aspire to. Here is why: True capitalism, by definition, does not exist anywhere. I do not know that it ever has. We willingly cede certain of our freedoms to government - any government - and we have for eons. What we have at most, is consensual capitalism by the_majority. Western societies have evolved, to where there are relatively few "haves", and a large and growing number of "have-nots." This cannot and will not be sustainable much longer. Either those who are in positions of power and influence adopt a more compassionate and humane form of capitalism by choice, or government, empowered by its financially disenfranchised electorate, will give it a mandate to do so, via the enforcement of laws.

FAITH AND REVOLUTION

When one first reads or hears the word revolution, thoughts of discord, lawlessness, blatant disregard for the rules of law emerge. That is not what this section is about at all. What it does point out is the following: the economic, environmental, social and political fabric of our world, insidiously, has become fragmented, and is becoming increasingly compromised. At one time, opposing political views were ones of disagreement. They have now been replaced with a venomous and toxic disagreeable spirit. At one time, the attaining of "the American Dream," was a viable reality for all those who were willing to make the attendant sacrifices, and work toward the goal. Today, barriers have been erected, to protect the few extremely financially fortunate, and to diminish the prospect, of them being toppled from their lofty stations. They are referred to as the "job creators."

There was a day when our national treasures were considered revered. Whether they were our state parks, the delicate economic and life-giving sustainability of our waterways, or the impact on livelihoods of the locals, as well as on animal creation and protection, they were to be guarded from all assailants. Today? "Drill, baby, drill." After all, we need to be protected from those greedy Middle East oil sheiks, don't we? Never mind that we import more oil from Canada than from any other country and Saudi Arabia is third after Mexico. What a ruse!

While the gains made for equality, regarding the gay/lesbian/bi-sexual/trans-gender community is laudable, those gains are continuously tenuous, fragile, and under assault from religious extremists of all colors and creeds. Recently, a Pastor on the evangelical religious right, stated that they should all be executed! I do not know what Jesus, this Pastor is in cahoots with, but it is not the Jewish one, of actual history. If that Pastor owned a bar or a restaurant, he would probably throw Jesus out on a dress code violation.

We need the kind of revolutions that sparked the Women's Suffrage Movement, and gave them a voice. The same voice that fueled the American Revolution, and gave birth to a nation, now freed from the dictates of a tyrannical oppressor an ocean away, thereby providing acceptance and protection for a whole disparaged segment of society. The African-American Civil Rights Movement, outlawed racial discrimination, and provided for those citizens, the right to vote. In addition, the American Gay Rights Movement spurred recognition of those individuals' dignity as members of humankind. All of mankind has been the most fortunate beneficiary, of these types of revolution. It is on these examples that I make my case.

I trust this sampling of themes we are going to consider together, has wetted your appetite. As we go for a deeper dive into each subject, I am going to lay all of my cards on the table, as to why I feel as I do. Much of what I will be sharing comes from my own, oftentimes painful, yet necessary experiences. You are going to get a 20/20 view of who I am. Through this process, you will be invited to carefully and quietly, reflect on how <u>you</u> view the same matters. I will be asking you to have the courage, to question some positions you have held, perhaps for most of your life. Some questions will result in your challenging long-held traditions. Perhaps, some of them <u>require</u> challenging!

Be brave! You and I are not here on this walk together by accident. This is a defining moment in your life. It is certainly a defining time globally. Most encounters have a beginning and an end, but not this one (at least not in that order). Our walk has an ending and <u>then</u> a beginning! The beginning will be obvious to you, when we conclude our journey together. For now, I am going to invite you to envision all of the themes that we will be encountering, with two words - THE END! In other words, to maximize our time together, it will be important to "deep-six" your prior experiences, prejudices, things you think you know, traditions, and to open yourself up to whatever El Elyon, the GOD MOST HIGH, wishes to impart to you. What you are about to undergo, if you will simply trust my counsel, is unfathomable as to its value.

✡ ✡ ✡

Beginning.

Here is something worth contemplating for a moment: "What beginning am I talking about?" I believe the answer is of the most profound nature. It is a great and mysterious question that has been, and will be, hotly debated for millennia to come. If you will allow me to wax religious for a moment, some people believe, as I do, that all things were initially created by DIVINE design and by the ONE who always was and always will be. For clarification, I do not align myself with religion, but rather with matters of faith. Divine Design strongly suggests that this CREATOR had no concrete beginning that we can point to and say, "Aha! There is the exact beginning. There is the CREATOR'S exact moment of beginning."

Beginning must therefore, stretch infinitely backward and infinitely forward, as there can be no line in the sand that delineates a precise beginning. Perhaps creation was always and forever in the heart and mind of the CREATOR. To deepen our understanding, if we have been created in HIS image, with many of the same attributes, it should follow, that all of our beginnings are only a measure, to ascertain the progress we have made from our last beginning_point! The term "beginning" should just serve as a way to measure our infinite growth and progress, nothing more. The word "beginning" should appear as simply recognizable, and be easily erasable in order to be replaced, with the next" higher beginning."

Therefore, while it is of great importance to rejoice in our progress, resting on the laurels of that progress for too long is a death sentence, when it comes to fulfilling the experience of our highest inheritance, which is living the infinite fullness of our life's journey. Following this train of thought, leads us to the conclusion, that the universe is continuously being created and designed, as part of a grand master plan, by the GRAND MASTER – that it's a constant work in progress. We should be pursuing the same unending joy of creation in our own lives.

Robert K. Cooper, Ph.D., in his book *Get Out of Your Own Way: The 5 Keys to Surpassing Everyone's Expectations*, stated: "The more you know or think you know about something, the more blinded you can be to what is actually happening."

This type of thinking has been referred to as "educated incapacity." The authors Chip Heath and Dan Heath, of the magnificent marketing book, *Made to Stick*, refer to this as "The Curse of Knowledge".

The Pulitzer Prize winning historian David Boorstin wrote, "The greatest obstacle to progress is not ignorance, but the illusion of knowledge."

The longshoreman-turned philosopher Eric Hoffer said, "In times of change, learners will inherit the Earth, while the knowers will find themselves beautifully equipped, to deal with a world that no longer exists." How tragic to invest one's time, talents and treasures in "a world that no longer exists."

This occurs every single day on a global scale, and is practiced by millions. Whether spiritual or secular, from small sole proprietorships, to multi-national corporate giants, by the masses and their advisors that make up the global population, this mindset has become the rule. Therefore, when I use the word "beginnings", it is **this fresh understanding** that I wish to convey, throughout the entirety of this manuscript. What I have in mind, is what has been referred to as a "beginner's mind."

I first encountered this revolutionary phenomenon, at a conference I was speaking at in Santa Monica, California. I was the first speaker, and after I spoke, the next speaker began his comments, by introducing the audience to the concept, of a "beginner's mind." He invited us to approach the balance of the meeting, with a mind-set that implied that we had never been exposed, to any of the material or concepts that were to follow. To be open to the notion, that it was fresh and new to us in every way imaginable, and that we were in unchartered territory. He went on to encourage the attendees, to create a space around each of our minds and hearts, which I call an inviolate sanctuary, wherein nothing could penetrate.

What followed throughout the balance of the conference, literally changed my life forever - personally, professionally and financially. Perhaps you have heard the term "deep listening." The concept of a "beginner's mind," takes the art of listening, to a place you possibly have not visited before. This is a space where deep and intense change, can and will take place. It is where ageless truth and wisdom are able to be heard. It is within. It is where the art of establishing a foothold to move toward your abundant future begins to take root. Imagine the energy, the anticipation, the mystery and adventure, if we approached everything from the perspective of a "beginner's mind!" What would the impact be on our most cherished relationships, on our chosen careers, our learning, our faith, on our fear and ignorance of one another, and our world? Limitless and unfathomable is an apt response.

It is also of great importance to be <u>present</u>. I do not mean to be physically in attendance. I mean to choose to constantly honor the reality of every moment we have together, so that your best creative responses can flow out of each and every instance. What you see on television and on the motion picture screen - however entertaining - is not reality. However, this very moment in time, this exchange - right now – is real. In fact, it is the only thing that is real. We need to revere and value every moment. Your highest progress demands this mind-set. If you want to experience, significant lifelong progress, and continually make a positive difference no matter the pursuit, "being present" is absolutely required.

This book is an invitation, for you to embark upon a journey unlike any other. Most trips have a start, middle and known finish point. There is an expected end in mind, and we typically pack appropriately for the trip. This is not the kind of journey I have in mind for you. This is an open-ended experience with no final destination at all! There is no finish point. It is an exhilarating journey into the unknown and is virtually impossible, to pack for in advance. In fact, the less you bring along at the beginning of your personal genesis, the better!

There will be moments, when you will doubt your resolve to continue. You will encounter resistance, both internally and externally. You might wonder if your sojourn at the moment should be made permanent. The portion of the brain that strives to keep you from advancing further, will whisper to you that the status quo is good enough, that you have progressed sufficiently, and that you are to be commended for even having the courage to start. It will remind you that you are shooting too high, and that at this stage of your life, it is no longer required, or even appropriate to stretch yourself.

Will you, like countless others before, succumb to that voice that bids you to settle for so much less, than the truths you were created to lay claim to? Will you fall short of your highest calling? Or will you join with the unique few, who commit to the notion, that the appearances of limitations and obstacles are really nothing more than the seeds that lay the foundation for your next awareness breakthrough? I request you to be amongst the committed ranks that confidently proclaim, "I have been created for greatness, to make enormous changes for good in my world. I am convinced that my greatest moments, are yet before me!"

Are you confident that your present self, is a mere shadow of what is to come? If so, I am excited and honored to be your personal escort on this journey, and am ready to leave whenever you are. I will meet you on the first page of Chapter 1. Pack lightly!

✡ ✡ ✡

Note: At strategic points along our journey, I will invite you to rest and quietly reflect on what we have just considered together. These are powerful opportunities to experience a personal breakthrough, an epiphany. I refer to these as "Rest Stops." You will be encouraged to simply STOP reading, put the book down (or stop the CD), and quietly ponder and reflect upon what has been presented to that point. Regarding the topic at hand, what do you now believe to be the truth of the matter? Do you view things the same way, or are you not as confident in the position you've held? By the way – what is the basis for that position? Is it a result of the research, quiet reflection, analysis, prayer and meditation that you painstakingly underwent yourself, or is it based on the views of someone else, including those of your family – that is, it's been passed down? If that be the case, perhaps it's really their position, a part of their legacy, being carried on through your life and your lips. It's extremely important that you are completely present, that you choose to shut out all unconscious thought, before you should expect to start receiving the answers, to what you have had the courage to question. These answers are a true reflection of where you are at this point in time. I cannot overstate the importance of this approach. This will make the difference, between this being just another book you have read or CD you have listened to, and a life-changing manifesto, that will provide continual progress, in every important area in your life. Of prime importance, is this journey will result in the discovery of your own life_purpose. Please take advantage of these opportunities.

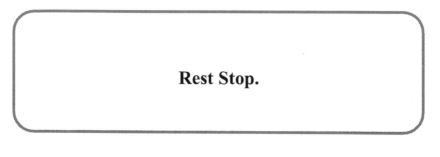

Rest Stop.

THE END!

Let's start walking!

THE WALK®

CHAPTER 1

WALKING on a SOLID FOUNDATION

Congratulations and welcome! It is so very good to see you again. I see that you have packed lightly, and trust you have conditioned yourself to have a "beginner's mind," as well as to be truly present, for the duration of our time together. You should be interested and excited to know, that I have done the same. Please know that your current thoughts and belief system, will try to force themselves into your mind and heart, as these have been practiced and reinforced by you and others for quite a while. It has become habitual. They will invite you to indulge and reinforce them. You must resist the temptation. Eventually, this chatter will speak to you with less frequency and intensity, being replaced by a more healthy way of being.

Aristotle correctly said that, "We are what we repeatedly do Excellence, therefore, is not an act, but a habit." What a tremendously self-empowering and exhilarating statement! The new habits that you form and have full control over, will powerfully position you for the rest of your life.

I am so excited to be accompanying you on this journey, as your teacher and coach. My confident expectation is that we will both be experiencing consistent progress, some planned for and some not! The unexpected progress and insights are the real special treats. They are all a part of your very own path. Taking this journey, could be the most important decision at this point in your life. All progress begins by telling the truth. An honest evaluation of where you are, in relation to a whole host of <u>big rock</u> issues is mandatory. This is where deep, creative thinking begins. I understand that telling the truth about something or someone in our life, can be extremely difficult, immobilizing and even painful. I wish there was a way to make real progress in these matters without this price. Yet, like most things in life, there is no free lunch here either.

Over the course of my life, of all the various and weighty subject matters that have crossed my path, a much smaller number rise to the top and represent <u>key markers,</u> in the ongoing manifestation of my life story. In every case, my own personal journey has gone from one of having "all the answers," to having more questions than answers! I have been changed from emotional immaturity, insensitivity, intolerance, self-righteousness, judgmentalism, ineffectiveness and pride, to choosing to have a "beginner's mind" in all things. At one time, my cup was so full, there was no room for anything more to be learned or experienced, and then I evolved to that of an empty vessel. There now exist unlimited room, for whatever I need in each moment to reach out to me, so progress can again be made. Each new experience brings me one step closer to my supreme worth. My posture in life has been radically altered, in ways I could never have foreseen. It continues to change and grow to this moment, in absolutely profound ways.

I am a work-in-progress, and I invite you to become the same. I truly believe this to be an essential ingredient, and inviolable truth for lifelong progress. This way of life, will lead you to discover your highest purpose.

As we walk, I would like to share my journey and my passions with you, regarding matters of faith and relationships, homosexuality, politics, capitalism, and revolution. As I let you in on the path I have traveled to this point, I am going to be thoroughly transparent to you. I will lay myself bare, and be an open book. My desire, is that you will not judge me, and will remain fully open with a "beginner's mind," from start to finish. My objective is to challenge you to challenge, what you think you already know and to empty your cup, of all-that-so-called knowledge. It is this pretense of knowledge that is keeping you from finding your path, and your key, to a

lifetime   of   ever-increasing   personal   significance,
abundance and happiness.

THE WALK®

CHAPTER 2

FAITH and RELATIONSHIPS
Back then when I knew it all.

I think it is important for you to know, that I am Jewish. As a child, I grew up in a fairly liberal "reformed" Jewish household. Every now and again, whether through something I read or heard in a conversation, I was confronted with a question, that would change my life for the rest of my earthly walk. The question was "Who was Jesus of Nazarcth?" Was he a wonderful man with great intentions, yet horribly self-deccived as to whom he was? Was he a brilliant con artist and manipulator, who knew exactly what he was doing, while deceiving many? Or was HE the promised Messiah of Israel, the ONE who has existed from the beginning of all beginnings, the anointed SON of GOD?

These burning questions were answered for me in 1982, when I was drawn to several great academic writings that carefully laid out the historical evidence I needed to support a position, one way or the other. To this day, I believe, with all of my heart and soul, that

Yeshua Ha-Mashiach, Jesus of Nazareth, is the Jewish Messiah. That is a personal belief, I quietly hold close to my heart, but am more than willing to share with those that inquire. Why am I telling you this?

My initial "Hebrew-Christian" experience was in the fundamentalist Evangelical camp, and oh, what a baptism I had! The initial spiritual grounding I received, which my mentors then believed to be most important, was lavishly heaped upon me without limit. Some of those early teachings are a significant part of who I am to this day. (Thank you, Wayne Sproule). My thirst for knowledge was unquenchable. I voraciously devoured great literary works, one after another, which supported the <u>absolute truth</u>. This studying supported what I thought, was pure, unalterable, and totally conclusive. This meant that, by default, anything and anyone that differed from <u>my</u> truth, was simply wrong. My understanding of correct doctrine was, at that time, irrefutable.

I could tell you with absolute confidence what religions represented a cult; what the final post-life destination was for the gay/lesbian community and how GOD viewed them (it was not pretty); the role of women in the family as seen through the eyes of the DIVINE; how animals figured into the big picture; and even the political party HE favored. Do not laugh – I was 100% serious. I could tell you, based on <u>your</u> doctrine, whether what you believed spiritually was correct. If not, I knew exactly where you needed to shape-up! I also knew whether you were truly saved (that is, deemed to be acceptable in the presence of a HOLY GOD). The list of my "knowingness" goes on, almost ad-infinitum. Why, I even truly believed the CREATOR was fortunate to have me on the team. I was the "Custodian of the Faith", "the gatekeeper of all that was good, pure and true."

Within weeks of my "spiritual awakening," I was asked to play the lead role in a cantata. that was being put on by Toronto, Canada's largest church fellowship. I am an accomplished vocalist, and was excited to discover that the performance would be broadcast nationally. Can you even begin to imagine what I was experiencing? New to the spiritual neighborhood, being cast in the highest profile role of this nationally broadcast cantata, in this multi-thousand member mega-church and, I am Jewish!

Based on fundamentalist Evangelical doctrine, being Jewish generally is a big deal. Being Jewish and accepting Jesus as the Messiah, can make you a Super Star, even a SUPER JEW in some settings. This was one such setting. I was so full of myself, so filled with the sense of my own holiness and godliness. My saintly radar was finely honed. I was ready to pounce, at the mere whiff of any devout impropriety. I had become the keeper and the defender of all that was worth defending. Everyone (and I mean <u>everyone</u>) wanted to meet me, touch me, pray with me, and break bread with me. Get in line folks. I was HOT!

A series of events such as this was perfect, for one who needed to have a genesis experience or, in other words, to begin all over again. Although I had just started all over again in matters of faith, I was lost in the wilderness of my own ego. But, I was certainly not going to be the one to bring about that metamorphosis. After all, I was GOD's gatekeeper. I had a reputation to protect! I desperately needed to have a date with the ONE, who cared enough about me, that HE would do what needed to be done to "right my ship," and clear away the trash I had accumulated. I was the one with the 2x4 in my eye. Everyone else had merely slivers.

I was about to experience a violent but necessary yanking of my divine carpet, from under my totally ego-made, imagined, rock solid foundation. I had no idea just how far I was about to fall. I will never forget that evening.

✡ ✡ ✡

So what was the most important thing GOD did in your life last year?

So there I was, meeting with other super-spiritual men and women who were also "on fire for GOD." We met every Friday evening at this small church, not far from my home. I was relatively new to "the faith", a Rock Star in the eyes of many (at least those that I thought mattered), semi-idolized by the Pastor of one of Canada's largest and most influential Evangelical churches, fresh from my theatrical cross-country televised exposure, imbued with the only right theology and filled completely with myself. If Lake Ontario wasn't so cold at that time of the year, I would have sworn that I could have walked on it.

Over the prior several months, a few well-intentioned friends of mine, had been feeling "lovingly compelled" to share with me, what my role as the man in our home entailed and, by extension, what my wife's role as the woman in our home **demanded.** (I have bolded the word "demanded" when referencing my wife to make a very important point).

These friends were replete with all the religious fervor and scriptural backing they could muster. What would any new man on the spiritual block do with all these "weapons" of love? What would a true child of GOD do with all that had been entrusted to him? The weight of the DIVINE responsibility was barely manageable! I imagined that the man of the family (me), in his new spiritual role, would tell_his wife precisely what her role required of her. After all, that was my duty. Her duty was simply to obey, that is, if she was going to be a GODLY woman. I had been told I was the spiritual head of my household and I reminded her of that fact regularly. I admonished her thoughtlessly, coldly, pride fully, and forcefully - in a spirit of love of course!

It didn't take long, before my actions, attitude and words, had destroyed her very spirit, and virtually the last drop of any remaining feelings of love she had for me. I had drained her emotional bank account. Our relationship's darkest hour had begun to unfold. We were nearing rock bottom in every way imaginable. The dike which was my newly found spiritual life had sprung a leak and was rupturing. All of my posturing that had played out for all to see and hear was about to be unveiled for the sham and thinly veiled pretense with little substance, that it truly was.

On this one particular Friday evening, the person who set the tone for the Friday "spirit-filled" get-togethers I had been regularly attending, thought it would be a good idea for us all to form a circle with our chairs, then go around the circle and share with the rest of the group, the most personally meaningful thing, that GOD had done in our lives the past year. I wanted to run away as far and as fast as I could. My marriage was in tatters and hanging on by a thread. My wife and I had become uncomfortably comfortable, with finding new and imaginative ways to hurt each other. We fought and aimed for the other's jugular. Although the spiritual front I was carrying around, was still in place, all be it, tenuously, my private life was an utter disaster. I knew it in every cell of my body. More importantly, GOD knew it, and HE was not going to let me off the hook that evening.

Each person shared, and as my time to do so was drawing closer, my heart began pounding. It felt as if it would explode right out of my chest. I had decided in advance, that when my turn to speak came, I would dig deep, and enthusiastically spew out some empty shallow narrative, that enabled me to continue to live the lie I had been living for some time. Why not? These people did not need to know my private business and, after all, they all held a lofty view of me. Why disappoint them?

What happened however, was not what I had planned for. As soon as it was my turn to share, I felt the rug begin to pull out from beneath me. Actually, I mean the rug, the broadloom, the linoleum, the tile, everything that had been undergirding the house of glass that I had been living in for months, was yanked away. The wind had been removed from my sails and I knew it. I broke down in an uncontrollable deluge of tears, screaming out, "I am the worst husband on the face of the earth." What followed, was probably the most important and life-giving statement of all – "I do not know how to do this. I do not know how to be a good life partner," I cried out in the presence of all. Those tears began a major healing. They were tears of blessed redemption.

The charade was over; the cat was out of the bag. All of my dirty laundry was in full view. I was standing naked. Despite all the self-righteous indignation I had been espousing, eager at the drop of a hat to tell anyone, what they needed to do to clean up their lives, and their relationships, my own backyard was a wasteland. Now everyone knew it. Thank GOD they did.

That night changed my heart forever, from the inside out. My attitude, what I believed in, and what I held as sacred in so many areas of my life, were now just shattered pieces. I knew I had to begin anew in every area of my life. This wasn't something a band-aid could heal. This required DIVINE heart surgery. Given the immense chasm that had developed in my relationship with my wife, and the tenuous state of our marriage, I knew clearly that this had to be my number one focus and priority. This is where I needed to make amends, and begin anew.

✡ ✡ ✡

From having all the answers, to having more questions than answers.

I had experienced a DIVINELY led cleansing. I came home from the meeting that night, entirely emptied of the things that had brought my marriage to the edge of the cliff. The spirit of "knowing it all" had been replaced by one of humbleness. Where pride in my rote memorization of holy writ, and my ability to retain vast amounts of "correct theology" was only hours removed, I began to seek and ask with honesty and true sincerity. The head knowledge now had a knowing heart. Legalism had been replaced by GRACE that was alive. Foolish and impotent GOD-less pride, had been poured out in a sea of tears and was now replaced by a GOD-honoring humility, one that provided a foundation for genuine healing. Falling to my knees in despair began a journey of real progress and a deepening relationship with my life partner and my **CREATOR**. The need for control and independence was replaced by a fervent desire for genuine relationship, and inter-dependence.

"May I speak with you for a few moments?" I asked my wife, shortly after getting home that night.

Understandably, she was on her guard immediately. She had been bearing up under the life-draining demands of listening to sermon after sermon, when I returned home from getting "filled with the truth." I had believed my role was to lead according to that truth, and her role, was to simply and obediently listen and follow, without question or comment. This had been a certain death of the soul – her soul. Reluctantly and miraculously, she agreed to listen one more time. This time however, the message and its tone were much different. For the first time since my initial spiritual awakening, the **SPIRIT OF THE HEAVENLY** was beginning to be in control, not me.

"I came to see this evening that I have been a terrible example of a husband to you, a horrible life companion, and not reflecting at all what GOD intends. My understanding of love and loving relationships has been diametrically opposed to DIVINE intention and purpose. I cannot believe how cruel, insensitive, and controlling I have been. I do not know how to do this right, but I am determined and committed to learn. I really want our marriage to work. I fully accept my share of the blame for where we are, which is probably all of it. Will you please forgive me?" I begged.

"I'll think about it," she replied. "And while I am thinking about it, I need you to honor my space. You've wounded me deeply and you will only make matters worse, if you try to get close before I am ready."

I responded, one last time, naively and insensitively, "How long will it be before you will be ready?" Reflecting back, this was not unlike the emotional immaturity of a 2-year old who asks, "Are we there yet?" when heading out on a long road trip, just moments into the journey. Immediately, I saw from her demeanor, that I was rushing things and needed to back off at once. I needed to allow her the time to say, "I will let you know when I am there, and when I have arrived."

When anything is acquired cheaply, including forgiveness, the lessons, and value, do not take root deeply, are not learned well and are destined to be repeated. The Path of real TRUTH always demands a price. It's simply not free! I told you this at the beginning of our walk together.

At that time, I wanted and needed to touch her, to receive some affirmation from her. I wanted some confirmation that I had touched her at some level. Realistically, that was as good as it was going to get for me that evening. Thankfully, I read the signs, and reluctantly did what turned out to be the wisest thing I could have ever done for our relationship. I respected her needs and feelings before my own. I should have been doing that from the beginning. I backed off and the need to begin again was born.

✡ ✡ ✡

Life after starting over and over and over again.

Great relationships are always a work in progress. They require continuously delving deeper planting, and trusting. The truly iconic relationships were forged and tried, by the trials of investing time in life's furnace. It is a series of two steps forward and one step back, although sometimes what is required, is one step forward and two steps back. Overall, with a sold-out commitment to the relationship's future success, incremental progress is made. A master sculptor was once asked how he created such magnificent works of beauty. He replied that he would begin with a block of marble, envision what the final result would look like, and then chip away, piece by little piece, until what remained, was what he had initially foreseen. Creating a masterful relationship is no different.

There are critically important pieces to this all-important puzzle that I would like to share with you. Dan Sullivan, *The Strategic Coach®* co-founder, cites two different kinds of people in the world: *Rugged Individualists* and *Unique Ability® Team Players*. A rugged individualist is one who truly believes he does not need anyone else in his life, to become all that he can be. What he does not know or possess today, he will acquire in time. He acts as if he can call upon his own sense (which is error-filled) of being omnipotent, omniscient and omnipresent at will (although he will deny that he believes he possesses these divine attributes). He is the sum and substance of himself, and believes that to be sufficient. He looks at himself in the mirror, and sees all that he will ever require. He is fully satisfied.

Little does he know, that what looks back at him, is a snapshot of his own shortcomings and a limited future; a future that pales immensely as to what could have been, his full potential. The borderline relationship (with the emphasis on the word borderline) with his life partner, if not already there, is moving steadily towards mediocrity at best, and a train wreck at worst.

Unique Ability® Team Players, on the other hand, know that they are not all things to all people. They also know they are not all things to themselves.

These people are the sum of all the wisdom, strengths, experiences, insights, and unique abilities of themselves and others. They joyfully embrace the importance of team. They know that there is no "I" in team and that a true partnership/relationship, involves two. They go on to become more than they could ever have become, by relying solely on themselves. They know that the borders, fences, and constraints of their own self-limits would impede their growth. When they look in the mirror, what looks back at them is a true collective, a joint work, a shared masterpiece, a tour-de-force and a powerful catalyst, for an ever deepening experience. This is the antithesis of what is represented by the rugged individualist. The team player becomes a shared third person in all of their relationships.

The *Jewish Scriptures* (also known as *The Older Testament*) portray this beautifully in Genesis 2:24, where the reference is made to two people in relationship becoming one. That one ought to be a cooperative, made up of the unique abilities of each. I can say, without reservation or hesitation, that the person I am today, am becoming tomorrow and forever thereafter, is primarily due to an acknowledgment and acceptance of this truth.

By opening my heart and mind, to fully receive the blessings of others' unique abilities to unite with my own, makes me much fuller and whole. It is not a sign of weakness as imagined by the rugged individualist – it is a sign of strength – and wisdom. Most notably, my wife Fran has been, and continues to be, the greatest contributor to my spiritual growth and life journey. I have been the beneficiary of her unique abilities for years. I would not have become even a modicum of who I am today, without her as my life partner. Thank GOD for those "pulled magic carpet" experiences!

I believe this is a good place to take a rest. As we settle here, relax and let me invite you to get present and reflect on some things. Where are you in your faith-journey at this time? Where are you generally, as to matters of faith and, specifically, as to your most valued relationships? Is your relationship with GOD an academic one, a relationship primarily of the mind? Is your relationship one, where you are proud of all the facts and information you have accumulated and are eager to share with others, so they can see also the truth (that is your truth) of your religion? Or is your relationship one of reverent questioning, struggling, and even daring to disagree? When was the last time you changed your mind about a matter of faith, you once held as inviolate? Have you become a closed book?

The CREATOR is big enough to handle your questions as well as your answers. Your relationship with HIM will not be in any jeopardy whatsoever. Do not allow anyone to convince you otherwise. His GRACE runs deeper than you can humanly imagine, literally. It is worth remembering that it was GRACE alone (and nothing else), that was the catalyst for the first beginnings of your faith-journey. GRACE was your divine invitation to enter into relationship with the ETERNAL, and faith alone that has brought you to this point. It was and continues to be an act of the SPIRIT, and not of the mind.

Regarding your most valued relationships: if you believe that you are the divinely appointed head of your household, do you also believe you have license to wield a big stick, to enforce your dictum and authority? Does this position allow you to verbally, physically, emotionally abuse your companion in order to empower your own shortcomings and weaknesses? Does it give you the right to avoid confronting what lurks in the darkness, out of the view of all but HIM? Remember, I am not judging you or your responses. Given my history, I am in no position to judge anyone. <u>All progress begins by telling the truth – remember?</u> Think about this for as long as you need.

Being divinely appointed as head of the household, should be viewed as a sacred duty. It is a privilege to carry out a time-honored responsibility, to honor one's life partner, and is to be approached and performed, with deep and abiding reverence and care. In all matters of personal choice and decision-making which will impact one's partner, the focus should always be on making the decision that affirmatively answers the question: "Does this sincerely reflect, what is in the best interest of my equal half and both of us together?" This is about how you adjudicate your highest calling.

Here is the good news. You do not have to figure out how to do this effectively by yourself (there is that rugged individualist rearing his/her head again)! You do not have to have a gut-wrenching personal encounter with GOD (as I did) to get the point. There are plenty of worthwhile resources. Are you ready for this? Your life partner possesses unique abilities different from yours, and if you are willing to listen and to act on their genius, she/he can be one of your most important sources for growth. You can then become an empowered team player, and a model of what HE has in mind, when head of household is referred to. If you listen deeply, she/he will tell you much of what you need to know. The application is up to you. Remember, this is about relationship, not control. It's about interdependence, not independence.

Rest Stop.

THE WALK®

CHAPTER 3

FAITH and the GLBT COMMUNITY
(GAY, LESBIAN, BI-SEXUAL, TRANS-GENDER)

Are you ready to continue? I hope you took all the time you required to carefully reflect on where you are, regarding your most valued relationships. The operative word here is relationship. I pray you have been honest with yourself in answering the questions. Let me repeat once again: this is a journey and a process. It's all about making incremental progress over time, as a result, of making effective life decisions. It's the finished work that matters. Do you remember the example given of how to create a masterful sculpture? You envision the final product first, and then you chisel away a piece at a time, until what remains, is the vision. This is also how great relationships are forged. They are master-filled relationships.

I would now like to speak with you about one of the most emotionally charged, controversial and polarizing topics of our generation. It's a subject so charged with passion, that families have been laid to waste because of it; longstanding fellowships have been torn apart. Where a faith-based relationship once existed, the "faith baby" has oftentimes been thrown out with the hate-filled and/or homophobic bath water. It's a theme so revolting to some, that they deem it a scourge upon the earth, and believe removal by whatever means is tantamount, to doing the mission of the HOLY ONE. This is a premise so inconceivable and appalling to some, that they spread their view with no regard to the fallout or how any listener would receive it. The messenger of this creed is deemed a person representing celestial authority (a pastor, for example). Because of this presumed authority, the recipient of the message can feel such hopelessness and despair, that the only solution is that of finality. We are seeing this played out in the world today, be they young or elderly.

What if the person who you are affronted by is just a child? What if that person is your child or your grandchild? How tragic unwarranted, appalling and needless that attitude would be. Such a contrary action this is to the message of true and unadulterated GRACE. GRACE is a missive of love and acceptance, without strings and conditions attached. There are no conditions on anything. GRACE implies a simple yet profound recognition, that all are created by and imbued in the image of the CREATOR. This is the spirit that does not judge, and acknowledges we are all subordinate to each other, and that everyone, with no exceptions whatsoever - regardless of their station in life, is superior to everyone else in some way. For example, the street person to a brain surgeon; a convicted criminal to a physicist; the elderly to the whiz kid, each individual possess a unique quality to be valued. And finally, a professional politician to the... okay, maybe there are some exceptions!

So where do you stand on faith and the homosexual? Is this question an oxymoron? Is it even worthy or appropriate of being in the same sentence or uttered in the same breath? That certainly was my posture at one time, back when I knew it all. When I encountered "the book", the manuscript that would be used by the ONE to literally change my heart, I also changed my views and my spiritual understandings. I began all over again.

✡ ✡ ✡

But first...

In retrospect, we really should not be terribly surprised at the prevalent attitudes toward the GLBT community. My sister-in-law Shein, who lived with us for years, had requested a family meeting of great importance. The attendees would be my wife Fran, our daughter Jennifer, Shein and me. I can visualize the scene as if it took place yesterday, yet as I reflect back, I only heard two words and they both pertained to our daughter: "I'm gay."

I do not remember saying anything at that moment. Fran cried quietly. I felt a mounting storm of holy anger beginning to emerge within me, and it was all focused on my sister-in-law, who had apparently known about this for a significant period of time, and who had the audacity, the gall to have kept it from us. How dare she? Did not she realize what she had willingly participated in? She was in concert with an unholy union. Our daughter was now condemned! She was certain to suffer a dismal future. What about the eternal abyss that would surely be her destiny? Was it all worth it, just so she could remain close with our daughter? I was absolutely convinced at that time, and for sometime thereafter, that my sister-in-law, was a champion for the dark side. She had easily compromised true faith. Listening to her defense of Jenn's chosen lifestyle and experiencing (what I perceived to be) her shallowness and weakness, repulsed me. I believed wholeheartedly that all Jenn needed, was to be divinely healed. This was a choice Jenn had mistakenly made. With GOD'S GRACE, she would choose to return to the light and be <u>normal</u>.

Little did I know that GRACE had other plans in mind, and they had more to do with me, than with Jennifer! Are you starting to see how this works?

✡ ✡ ✡

The Book.

How long the book rested on Fran's bedroom end table before I first noticed it, I do not recall. I do remember having noticed it out of the corner of my cye on occasion. All I know with reasonable certainty is that Fran probably had no intention of reading it, as she is more of a hands-on person in her approach to things. I have no insight as to who the intended reader was. Later on, Jenn said she did not recall either. What I do know for certain is that one evening, which became an evening of deep and personal historic significance; my eyes were clearly drawn to "the book." Its allure was unmistakable. What was its focus? What message did Jennifer want to convey to us, to me? What infamy did she want us to believe? It was I who knew the truth and nothing and no one was going to convince me otherwise (or so I thought). I picked the book up, got into bed, and started to read, and then read some more. I could not put it down. I felt like I was in the grip of some invisible force that would not let go, until it achieved its intended purpose.

To say that I was blindsided, is an understatement of the highest order. I was at the same time, both awestruck and energized. Sleep would not have its way for hours to come. It was eventual exhaustion that provided a respite from the DIVINE surgery, that was now fully in motion. Little had I realized that all my prayers for meaningful, deep life and heart change to be effected in my daughter Jenn, and my sister-in-law, were actually prayers being redirected right back to me. The DIVINE had a work of GRACE to accomplish in my heart. The weeds were flourishing in my own backyard in great abundance. It was <u>my</u> attention HE wanted. HE got it.

It has been said that timing is always perfect. The timing of when I began to read "the book" was absolutely in DIVINE order. It started a journey which continues to this day. Ah! Forgive me. It would be helpful if you knew the name of the book. It is called: *Is the Homosexual My Neighbor? A Positive Christian Response*, written by two longtime, extremely close friends: Letha Dawson Scanzoni and Virginia Ramey Mollenkott. Both of these amazing women are filled with devotion and faith. Virginia is a lesbian Christian who "came out" to Letha <u>after</u> they had begun the research, which became the foundation for their stunning book. Since my spiritual heart surgery, I have had the privilege and joy of recommending and gifting this powerful ministry of reconciliation and healing on many occasions.

✡ ✡ ✡

What about the Homo-Scriptures ("The Big 7")?

There is hardly a conversation one can have today, with a large segment of certain groups of faith on the topic of homosexuality, without them bringing up at least one, of what I have named the "homo-scriptures." There are <u>seven big ones</u>, which they hang their allegedly inscrutable dogma on. When one reads the cited references in plain English today, taking every word literally and possibly then mixes it with a healthy dose of prejudice and homophobia, their posture seems to be clear and indisputable. Do you have the courage to go deeper, and delve beneath the surface of what seems to be irrefutable truth? Are you willing to approach these same verses from an historical-critical perspective, one that takes into account both the culture and the language of a time in antiquity? If so, you are going to discover a whole new world. Much of what I'll be sharing with you, I first read in the outstanding work titled "What the Bible Really Says About Homosexuality" by Daniel A. Helminiak, Ph.D. I am indebted to Dr. Helminiak for his tireless work in this area.

So that you can refer to these verses yourself, "The Big 7" as referenced from *The New International Version of The Bible* are:

- Genesis 19: 4-13, [4] "Before they had gone to bed, all the men from every part of the city of Sodom —both young and old— surrounded the house.[5]They called to Lot, "Where are the men who came to you tonight? Bring them out to us so that we can have sex with them." [6] Lot went outside to meet them and shut the door behind him[7] and said, "No, my friends. Don't do this wicked thing.[8]Look; I have two daughters who have never slept with a man. Let me bring them out to you, and you can do what you like with them. But don't do anything to these men, for they have come under the protection of my roof." [9] "Get out of our way," they replied. "This fellow came here as a foreigner, and now he wants to play the judge! We'll treat you worse than them." They kept bringing pressure on Lot and moved forward to break down the door.

[10] But the men inside reached out and pulled Lot back into the house and shut the door. [11] Then they struck the men who were at the door of the house, young and old, with blindness so that they could not find the door. [12] The two men said to Lot, "Do you have anyone else here—sons-in-law, sons or daughters, or anyone else in the city who belongs to you? Get them out of here, [13] because we are going to destroy this place. The outcry to the LORD against its people is so great that he has sent us to destroy it."

A literal rendering of this account, would seem to be a blanket condemnation of homogenital acts. However, there is simply no way of clearly knowing, whether this text refers to homogenitality or not. What is certain is that this text is concerned about abuse, not simply about sex.

A cardinal rule of Lot's society was to offer hospitality to strangers. This was taken to such a degree, that no one might even harm an enemy who had been given shelter for the night. Lot refused to expose his guests, foreigners, to the abuse of the men of Sodom. This would have been a violation of the law of sacred hospitality, a matter of even greater import, as Lot too was not a native of Sodom.

The context of that day was also replete with the ultimate in humiliation – men forcing sex on other men. In war, besides raping the women and slaughtering the children, the victors also "sodomized" the defeated soldiers. What was in mind here was to insult the men, by treating them as women. The objection was more to a man's being "effeminate" than to his having sex with another man.

So what was the sin of Sodom? It clearly, was an abusive and offensive stance towards strangers and travelers, as well as an inhospitable-spirit towards the needy. That is the story of Sodom taken in its historical context. When male-male rape is introduced, sexual abuse takes center stage. Insult and humiliation wore the same cold, detestable, monstrous mask then as now. Numerous other biblical references to Sodom validate that her transgressions were many, but inappropriate sexual acts was just one. The Sodom story is simply not solely about sex. To employ the narrative to condemn homosexuality, is a blatant misuse and "stretch" of the Jewish Scriptures, and should be ceased immediately, by all, especially those who profess them as being DIVINELY inspired.

> Leviticus 18:22 22 "Do not have sexual relations with a man as one does with a woman; that is detestable" and Leviticus 20:13 13"If a man has sexual relations with a man as one does with a woman, both of

them have done what is detestable. They
are to be put to death; their blood will be
on their own heads.

Once again, a literal current day reading of these
scriptures would seem to be as clear as a bell as to their
meaning, that is, until you dive deeper. The
condemnation of homogenital acts occurs in a section of
Leviticus called "The Holiness Code," a litany of laws and
punishments required for Israel to remain "holy" in God's
sight. Ancient Israel was to be different from all the other
nations on the earth. They were to be a special people, set
aside, a people chosen to be HIS earthly ambassadors.

Male same-sex acts were prohibited for religious
reasons and not for sexual ones. Israel was to be separate
from the Gentile nations and not practice as they did. The
prohibition of male-male sex occurs only in The Holiness
Code of Leviticus and nowhere else. The intent was to
keep Jewish identity strong and separate. The big-rock
issue was one of religious exclusion and, not ethics or
morals.

The reason the Jewish Scriptures forbid male-male
penetrative sex has nothing to do with homosexuality
today. It had everything to do with purity, with
maintaining the ideal order of things, and not the
rightness or wrongness of the sex, in and of itself. The

objections cited in The Holiness Code within Leviticus, simply has no bearing today. Further, references to the words homosexual and heterosexual would have been totally foreign to the people of that day.

Finally, the word "detestable," is a translation of the Hebrew word toevah. The word zimah could have been used in its place. Zimah conveys an injustice – a sin. On the other hand, toevah means that which is ritually or culturally forbidden. If male-male sex is a sinful act, why didn't the author use the word zimah? Is it because the issue at hand was one of social and religious taboos and not one of sexual ethics?

- Romans 1:26-27 "Because of this, God gave them over to shameful lusts. Even their women exchanged natural sexual relations for unnatural ones.[27]In the same way the men also abandoned natural relations with women and were inflamed with lust for one another. Men committed shameful acts with other men, and received in themselves the due penalty for their error."

This passage from Romans is the most important statement on homosexuality in the Bible so I'm going to invest a fair amount of time addressing it – and it teaches that sex, whether heterosexual or homosexual – is ethically neutral. Here's the substance. The Greek words translated as "unnatural" are para physin and conveys the idea of acting contrary to one's nature and not necessarily, contrary to the laws of nature. Paul's usage of these words implies that something is natural, when it responds according to its own kind, when it is as it is expected to be. When someone did something out of character, they were acting unnaturally. Paul was stating that these men and women were engaging in sexual practices that were different from the norm. There is no suggestion whatsoever, that these practices were contrary to DIVINE order, that they were somehow wrong. They were simply different - atypical.

Does God act para physin – unnaturally, in the same way?

Apparently so! In Romans 11:24, Paul speaks of how God grafted the wild branch of the Gentiles, into the cultivated olive tree that is the Jewish people and therein lies the point. Normally, one would graft a branch of a cultivated tree into the stock of the wild tree. God did a new thing. He reversed the known order. It was unnatural. It was para physin. HIS ways are not our ways. HE will not be bound by our understandings or limitations. God had established a new order. All things had become as new. There was no longer Jew or Gentile, slave or free, male or female. Social distinctions and cultural categories were tossed out the window. If Paul meant that para physin, implied an act of immorality and moral condemnation in Romans 1:26-27, then by extension, he would also be saying that God is immoral, unethical, whimsical. The mere thought of that is patently absurd, and won't be entertained beyond my saying so here. What about the use of words shameful? This is the Greek word "aschemosyne" and it means "not according to form" in verse 27. Further, in its other uses throughout scripture, it never implies moral judgment.

Paul clearly had access to words that mean ethically wrong, sinful, but he deliberately chose not to use them when speaking of homogenital acts, Greek words like asebeia and adikia. They do however; appear in the sections just before and after the section addressing homogenital acts, but not within it. That said, it would be perfectly reasonable to assume, that wherever Paul speaks of homogenitality in Romans, he had the Jewish law in mind. After all, this is the much esteemed Rabbi Saul of Tarsus we're talking about here. Given his religious upbringing, and the close relationship in the ancient Hebrew world, between religious uncleanness and social dishonor, it should be entirely understandable for Paul to regard homogenitality as dirty, unclean, and impure, yet not an ethical condemnation, when writing to the Romans. Remember, the teachings of Leviticus had been indelibly engraved in his heart. Perhaps that's why the so-called modern translation of Romans, feels so much like Leviticus.

With the Rabbi Saul of Tarsus turned Apostle Paul, and his enlightened understanding of true purity issues, now viewed through the eyes of his beloved Messiah, why would he even raise issues of purity in this context? Paul wants to draw attention to a vast chasm of real distinction – those of ritual impurity and real wrong. In Romans, any reference to homogenital acts as being unclean, are unclean solely when viewed through the lens of ancient Jewish religious standards – principles that should have no place in today's culture, to say nothing of those who profess a faith in the ONE who declared all things as new. Those that fuel the hatred, oppression, and brutality toward the GLBT community, are the purveyors of disrepute on the message of DIVINE LOVE and GRACE. Men and women, who claim lives of genuine faith, ought to know better.

- 1 Corinthians 6:9-10 [9] "Or do you not know that wrongdoers will not inherit the kingdom of God? Do not be deceived: Neither the sexually immoral nor idolaters nor adulterers nor men who have sex with men[10] nor thieves nor the greedy nor drunkards nor slanderers nor swindlers will inherit the kingdom of God" and 1 Timothy 1: 9-10 [9] "We also know that the law is made not for the righteous but for lawbreakers and rebels, the ungodly and sinful, the unholy and irreligious, for those who kill their fathers or mothers, for murderers, [10] for the sexually immoral, for those practicing homosexuality, for slave traders and liars and perjurers — and for whatever else is contrary to the sound doctrine."

Here, we have another matter of great importance, if one is to understand what the author meant to convey in these passages (what I would give to be able to ask them), when it comes to homogenital acts, if anything, and it comes down to the interpretation of 2 hotly debated Greek words – malakoi and arsenokoitai. Malakoi has no specific reference to homogenitality whatsoever and arsenokoitai, while possibly referring to male-male sex acts, would condemn irresponsible homogenital acts but not homogenital acts in general. It seems that the interpretation of these 2 words, depends on what version of the Bible one chooses to endorse and the year it was published. Malakoi by itself has been interpreted as effeminate, soft. When taken together, these words have been translated as "homosexuals," or "sexual perverts." Taken separately, they have been interpreted as "male prostitutes and sodomites." Modern translations have rendered arsenokoitai as "homosexuals," 'sodomites," "child molesters," "perverts," "homosexual perverts," "sexual perverts," or "people of infamous habits" (my mother-in-law would have consistently accused me of this form of arsenokoitai). Malakoi has been interpreted as "catamites," "the effeminate," boy prostitutes" or even "sissies." Some would suggest the most accurate translation is "indulgent." Translations have indeed followed prejudices. Here is where the rubber meets the proverbial road: Nobody knows for sure what these 2 words mean. This is hardly a sound and just foundation on which to base the notion of an entire community sinning before God.

To import the word homosexuality into this argument imputes a psychological and sociological understanding of sexual orientation that simply, was foreign to the Christian world at that time. First-century Christianity looked disparagingly upon exploitative and wanton sex and not male-male sex in general. It's my contention, that the Bible affirms mutual respect, caring and sharing, wrapped up in relationships of true love – whether in a heterosexual or in a GLBT setting.

• Jude 1:7[7]"In a similar way, Sodom and Gomorrah and the surrounding towns gave themselves up to sexual immorality and perversion. They serve as an example of those who suffer the punishment of eternal fire."

This brief text, just like the majority of today's Biblical scholars who contend that the Sodom account had nothing to do with homogenitality, doesn't assert it here either. Again, scripture can be twisted in any number of ways, in order to validate one's posture, regardless of the basis for that view. The entire argument rests on two Greek words – sarkos heteras. The King James version of the Bible, may be helpful in assisting us to get a credible handle on the correct translation.

It reads: "Even as Sodom and Gomorrah and the cities about them in like manner, giving themselves over to fornication, and going after strange flesh, are set forth as an example, suffering the vengeance of eternal fire."

What is this "strange flesh?" Humans having sexual intercourse with angels – that's what! It's troubling when one realizes, that the 1989 "New Revised Standard Version of the Bible, in this verse, says "Sodom pursued unnatural lust, while the New American Bible says, "practiced unnatural vice" and The New Jerusalem Bible says, "Sodom was equally unnatural." The problem with these three translations is that nothing in the Greek text should be translated "unnatural." Just like in the Genesis 19 account, trying to litigate the matter of this text, as being one of DIVINE displeasure towards homogenital acts, is a classic "square peg in a round hole illustration."

I truly hope what I've had to say has been helpful, as you carefully consider your position on this extremely important matter. Questioning that which we have held to be irrefutable, takes chutzpah (having chutzpah conveys boldness coupled with supreme self-confidence). Even if these opposing and alternative views are dead wrong (which I believe would be quite a "stretch"), and the conservative modern day depiction is absolutely correct, ostracizing this community divides, excludes, shuns, judges and condemns. All these actions run contrary to reconciling with the heart of GOD, and are patently wrong. I'd like to share with you another rich experience I've had, regarding the GLBT community that deeply impacted me!

The Church Service.

My wife and I had been invited to a Sunday worship service in East Toronto several years ago, by gay friends of ours. Several things happened at that service that I have never forgotten. To begin with, I had seldom experienced a greater outpouring of genuine praise and worship to the ALMIGHTY, than the one we encountered that morning. The presence of HIS SPIRIT was palpable. Soon into the service, something happened that I could not have remotely expected. The Pastor, Dr. Brent Hawkes, in addressing his entire congregation, asked every gay or lesbian attendee to raise their hand, if by simply wishing it, they could be "straight," knowing they could not.

Pastor Hawkes' hand was raised amid the throng. I was speechless. One did not need to do a head count. The result was clear and overwhelming. Being straight was the choice by a landslide. Could it be that being homosexual was not a lifestyle decision, but was something beyond one's control? After all, who would choose to be an object of much derision, as unfounded as it is. To stretch my understanding of correct theology could this possibly be an act of DIVINE DESIGN? My entire foundation of faith, screamed out in opposition to such heresy and yet, I was witness to an outpouring, a transparent voicing of the hearts of many. Just when I thought the intensity of the service had reached its crescendo, and that it could not possibly rise beyond or deepen where we had been taken, it did.

A call went out to all those in attendance that were sick to come forward, to petition the healing hand of the ONE who is the bringer of miracles. A great number came forward with all manners of infirmities and in varying degrees. Some were temporal and already experiencing progressive healing, some were terminal - steadily and painfully heading towards their eternity. It was this latter group that arrested my attention and grabbed hold of my heart. It was a moment and an expression of what it means to be truly human. The mere recollection of this moment still touches my heart.

How can any person, let alone any person of faith, not choose to subordinate their theology and understanding of "correct" doctrine, no matter how it may not square up with someone else's, in the midst of such human distress? How can one so coldly and casually "play the sin card" (suggesting this is a HOLY GOD's judgment on the practicing homosexual)? Is it not GRACE alone that enables you, me, all of us to breathe our next breath? Even if conservative theology is absolutely correct in its posture towards homosexuality, do not we all fall short of the GLORY, the HOLINESS of GOD? Doesn't it say in *The Newer Testament,* that it is by HIS GRACE alone, that we are received into HIS HOLY PRESENCE, and not by any act or inaction of our own, hence having no basis for feeling self-proud? Don't we all blow it on a daily basis? Does DIVINE GRACE have qualifiers? Can it cover over our minor sins, but as to "The 7 Homo-Scriptures," are we pushing the divine envelope? I am persuaded that HIS GRACE is larger than all the judgments and completely beyond our comprehension.

As to the matter we've been discussing, I don't know where you currently stand, but wherever that may be; I am not asking you to change your mind as to your understanding of GOD's heart. That would be contrary to HIS intended design that we have free will. I am inviting you to change your heart, or more properly, to ask for HIM to perform DIVINE surgery where it may be required, so that, notwithstanding your theology, GRACE is delivered with a compassion for human inclusivity of all kinds. We all have a 2x4 in our eye which requires urgent and focused attention. I am inviting you to be an agent of GRACE, and not a catalyst for driving someone's child, grandchild, perhaps your own, ever deeper into "the closet," possibly reaching the point of utter despair, hopelessness and the wish to end their pain.

The service concluded with a magnificent and stirring vocal presentation of *For Those Tears I Died*, sung by Marsha J. Stevens, the creator of the lyrics. This GOD-honoring masterpiece and tribute to the CREATOR, appears in most hymnals in churches across North America and many parts of our world. The number of times that song has been chosen for a church service's praise and worship over the years, would count in the millions and continues to this day. Would you think less of this musical work of art, if you learned that Marsha is a lesbian Christian? Would the significance of the song's message somehow be less worthy? Would you, like some, tear its pages from your hymnal and ask for GOD's forgiveness, even though you were swept up to the heavenly realms as you sang it perhaps only yesterday? Well, she is a lesbian Christian and I truly hope you would not remove this intoxicating tribute to the DIVINE from your hymnal.

It is all about relationship.

I am not going down this road to disparage the conservative body of faith. I would then be just another hypocrite, and not one who is trying to "walk his talk." Most of the conservative adherents are followers of a body of truth they believe to be pure and unblemished. I understand that most of these people, in their defense of "this truth," are doing so out of a genuine love for their GOD and a sincere commitment, to protect the integrity of what they believe in. I commend them all for their steadfastness and resolve. Those are worthy traits. But even when we assume ourselves to be right, having the need to dogmatically hold onto and demand our position to be the only position, should never trump our relationship with that person. You can proclaim you are doing it because you care about that other person and their standing before GOD. You feel you must charge them, no matter how painful it might be for them, out of love. I used to have the same type of spirit.

Listen to me! The AUTHOR OF LOVE will bring about all the changes HE desires in everyone, even you!

HE will do it in HIS perfect time, not yours. HE will make the changes of HIS choosing, not yours.

So what is a lesbian doing in a Baptist conservative church?

Imelda was a student studying to be a professional sign language interpreter when my wife Fran was doing the same. They quickly became close friends. We enjoyed the times we would all meet for dinner in downtown Toronto. Those were special moments. We simply loved her for who she was. We could not have imagined or acted otherwise. Imelda is a gay woman of faith. On numerous Sundays, she would accompany us to a conservative Evangelical church service, where Fran was signing for the congregation's deaf. I will never forget how after one service, Imelda posed a question to me. I've recounted it many times since.

"Do you know why I come to these services with you both?" Clearly she knew the stance of most Evangelicals towards gays and lesbians! I saw her holding her copy of the Bible as she answered, "Because you accept me just as I am."

This is what the story of DIVINE LOVE and GRACE is all about: The INFINITE reaches down to the finite, the mortal, because of HIS deep desire for relationship with us, and nothing more. After all, what do we have to offer the AUTHOR of LIFE? What will we teach HIM? What will we correct HIM on? If righteousness was the standard, if suitability was the acceptable measure, who amongst us could stand and make the grade?

I have one last point to make and then we shall take a breather. We will be spending a long time with our gay, lesbian, bi-sexual and transgender brothers and sisters of faith on the other side, where all of this will not matter a whit. All of our prejudices, misguided senses of self-piety, and all else that divides and excludes will be gone forever. It would be a great idea to start getting to know them on this side first.

Let's rest here now and quietly reflect on those members of the GLBT community who we can reach out to and choose to do a better job in the area of relationship? Can we rest from the need and the servitude to be right, and simply honor others for who they are right now? The knowledge that we can will enable us to rejoice in the fact, that they too are made in the image of the CREATOR, just like us? All of us – all of mankind – is comprised of individuals, one-of-a-kind, matchless gems.

Rest Stop.

THE WALK

CHAPTER 4

FAITH and POLITICS

GOD is not a Republican or a Democrat.

Let's continue our walk. Do you remember I said earlier that all of life should be a series of new beginnings, of starting over and having a spirit of deep listening? While we were resting just now, someone came to mind that I am sure I can learn much from, in an area that is very important to my larger future. I realized that I first needed to acknowledge his superiority over me in that field. I must reach out and validate him, establishing that I honor and value him and his unique abilities that are so different from my own. This not only opens a portal to my bigger future, it also serves to make progress in a longstanding languishing relationship.

I was having lunch with an Evangelical Christian friend of mine not long ago, and as we were heading back to his office, I asked him a question, I had wanted to ask him for quite some time. I always wondered why he has put his political support behind the Democrats these many years (in Canada this would be the Liberals, the

Social Democrats in the U.K., etc.), given that most conservative Christians do not identify with the Democratic Party in the U.S.

Without hesitation and not surprisingly, he said, "Because I believe that Jesus would have been a Democrat."

I could ask that same question of countless friends and clients and they would answer similarly, except they would insert the political party that reflects their own ideology: Because I believe Jesus would be a Republican, a Libertarian, and a Socialist." Different faiths would engender the same biased results, only the names would be changed. As I reflect on all of this, one overriding thought prevails:

GOD IS NOT A POLITICIAN.

It seems to me that any attempt on our part to align the DIVINE with a specific institutional entity that is made up of the frailties of mankind, is a faulty design of our own creation. Could that be the reason behind HIS WILL that we pray for our leaders? HE knows only too well the hearts and predispositions of all mankind, no matter their political and ideological leanings. I believe it is HIS creative intention that there are governmental institutions, ideally to carry out and be HIS ambassador for good purposes. Yet to humanize HIM, on a level that suggests HE backs and casts HIS vote towards one political party or the other, is patently absurd. GOD rejoices in <u>every</u> expression of those things that convey HIS HEART towards HIS entire creation. GOD wants us all to express compassion, mercy, grace, love, forgiveness, charity, humility, and stewardship, no matter who the messenger is, be they Republican, Democrat, Muslim, Jewish, Buddhist, etc. Why then do we have this mindset?

First of all, by creating this paradigm in our own minds - that the very heart of the CREATOR of the universe perfectly lines up with mine - enables and empowers us to concretely validate our own perspectives and platforms. If this is the case, would anyone even consider whether there exists another valid point of view? Doesn't *The Newer Testament* say, "If GOD is for us, who can be against us?" No one, I suppose. But if GOD is not with you as to certain political and/or social matters you cling to, what then?

Don't we now "see through the glass darkly?" This implies that no matter how certain we are as to the correctness of our platform; we are simply incapable of having our mindset affirmed with absolute precision and unqualified accuracy. To take a position that is so thoroughly resolute and steadfast, is tantamount to opening ourselves up to those very things that would distance us from the mind and the heart of the CREATOR. Such stances like conceit, pride, egotism and self-importance, take us away from the DIVINE. We all need to simply stop where we now stand on a whole host of issues and set aside some quality quiet time to allow for deep reflection. We then must ask ourselves some questions, and be willing to be honest with ourselves.

What do I believe as to a certain issue? Why do I hold this view? Am I truly open to an alternative perspective, to even starting over again? When all is said and done, is my stance GOD's stance? Is my heart HIS heart, or is there something else at play here and I have conveniently invited HIM, in name only, to come along for the ride to authenticate it?

It is my own personal conviction, that in order to make progress in any matter of great importance, we need those people whose views are divergent from ours. Ultimately, this progress will lead to relationship, and relationship draws us all closer to the purposes and the heart of GOD.

We are only too aware of the numerous atrocities that have been done, and continue to be done, allegedly in HIS NAME, whether crimes against humanity, HIS animal creation or the planet HE has entrusted to us in general.

My wife and I attended a church service some years ago that will stay with me forever. After the members of this church heard a tape recording of mine, I was asked to be the "special music" on this one particular Sunday morning. After the worship portion of the service concluded, the Pastor made some disparaging remarks about the work of the organization *Greenpeace*, and concluded by saying, "If GOD cared about the preservation of the whales and the alleged mistreatment of them, HE would do something about it HIMSELF. Therefore, the fact that this continues to be carried on under HIS watchful eye, is proof positive that it is a non-issue to HIM."

I suppose the same could be said for an uncountable number of daily atrocities that continue on a global basis. Think of the millions of insufferable lives that are subject to the hands of corrupt and murderous dictators, while those more fortunate plan their next vacation. Think of the number of animals who are bred to fight to the death, often their own, while those who hope to profit from their blood, look on without any regard whatsoever, for the torture being heaped upon GOD's living creations. These creations were entrusted to us to protect by GOD! Think of the barbaric trafficking in human beings, including children, as sex slaves under the accommodating eyes of local politicians and law enforcement on the take. Few ever escape with their lives. These souls were once filled with hope and innocence. They end up sullen, emptied, barely husks. They end where the hope of death is their only escape.

So if GOD cared about these and thousands of situations I could cite, would HE not do something about it HIMSELF? Isn't the fact that such atrocities continue to be carried on under HIS watchful eye, proof positive that these are all non-issues to HIM? What is my response to these questions? I will tell you.

There is a story in the Jewish Scriptures where GOD spoke through an ass (that is, a donkey). Notwithstanding the plain idiocy of that Pastor's comments regarding the treatment of whales, if we assume for a moment that this man was genuinely called by GOD to be the shepherd of a flock, it then becomes equally clear to me that GOD is still choosing to <u>speak through an ass</u>! (I have not been asked back to sing at that church). Phew! I am so glad I got that off my chest.

SO IF GOD CARES AT ALL, WHAT NOW?

I believe that GOD does care about the health and well-being of HIS entire creation, in ways and to depths we are incapable of understanding and experiencing fully. I also believe that HE has made it crystal clear over the years, as HE has moved powerfully and unmistakably in the hearts and minds of many men and women, what HE passionately desires from us. HE has chosen what the roles and responsibilities for us are as we work in harmony with HIM. Again, it is a <u>team</u> effort. To be clearer still, it is a <u>GOD</u> thing. This implies that HE fully empowers those doing His chosen work.

The Irish statesman, orator and politician, Edmund Burke (1729 - 1797) said, "All that is necessary for the forces of evil to win in the world, is for enough good men and women to do nothing." On the flip side, I am thrilled to pieces and feel amazingly empowered, as I reflect on the new realities that can be actualized when I re-state Mr. Burke's citation with a twist: If all that is necessary for the forces of evil to win in the world is for enough good men and women to do nothing, then it must logically follow, that all that is necessary for the forces of good to win in the world, is for enough good men and women -- <u>to do something</u>!

SO WHAT SHOULD THE GROUNDRULES
OF "SOMETHING" BE?

To begin, whatever that "something" is, it's going to be different from one person to another and it is going to be dissimilar as to its magnitude and the skill sets that will be required for success. Nevertheless, each one will be a meaningful contributor in effecting good in the world. One is not more important, more significant, or more vital than the other.

You may never know how the good seed that you planted at one time, regardless of how insignificant the act seemed to you, grew to become an enormous force in the world for effective change, decency, compassion, respect and virtue. Relationships that have a solid foundation, substance and bright future, are still entered into one at a time and are very personally customized to the needs of the recipients with that special something. Let me suggest to you what I believe some of the essentials are as you reflect on this matter. Before you do so however, it will be of prime importance that you embrace an unwavering commitment, to viewing all of GOD's creation as having innate worth and unlimited potential, thereby becoming a strategic partner in that vision and solution. This leads to all of creation achieving its intended highest purposes, a HOLY mission whose time is long overdue. The essentials are:

- The undertaking should flow from you as an unimpeded river, without reservation or hesitation. There should be no question in your mind and heart whatsoever, that the act is firmly in keeping with what you have been created to do at that moment in time, and requires no one's permission to move forward.

- There is no personal agenda, other than to be an agent of good in the world. There should be no desire or need for any form of self-promotion. In fact, the endeavor might be done out of sight of all but yourself, the beneficiary and the ALL SEEING ONE. It matters not who, if anyone, gets the recognition.

- It will require the unique abilities of others, if the highest results are to be achieved. You recognize and rejoice, in the fact that you have a few of these unique abilities and no more, and will need to call upon others whose specialized abilities are both different and complimentary to yours. This may require you to call upon best-of-class relationship building skills, as these team members may naturally approach a given task, very differently from you. They may even view the best route to accomplishment different from your own, which may be a reflection of their personal genius. Do not judge the value they can bring to the table by their economic and/or social status. Everyone, without qualification, is superior to everyone else in some way.

- Until you first own your emotions, you will never own your life, be it your present and/or your future. To claim your emotions, is to move forward with regular progress. To do otherwise, is to be continually pulled back to old, less effective and possibly destructive prior modes of behavior and past habits.

- You must arrest any need to be right (even when you are fully confident in your position), for nothing will destroy a relationship faster (and perhaps the good you are wanting to effect). It is the big picture, the passion for being a powerful agent of change, which is to be in clear focus and not our petty sensitivities and egos. When the entire team embraces and signs on to these ground rules, the power and the potential for change will be of epic proportions.

This is a fair amount to digest. Let's take a breather and reflect on one matter, where we have the zeal and enthusiasm to be an agent of change for good in the world. What are the next steps to bring this to pass, to commit to implementing the ground rules referenced a few moments ago, and the task at hand to achieve success?

Rest Stop.

THE WALK®

✡ ✡ ✡

CHAPTER 5

FAITH and CAPITALISM

What is it really, have we lost our way
and if so, can it be restored?

I do not know where you stand on this matter, but I have found myself saying of late that, "It's becoming increasingly tough for me to be a capitalist." I am uncomfortable with the brand of capitalism that has worked its way into much of society. The degree of irresponsibility, insensitivity, cover-up, greed and blatant disregard for all but a few, as exercised by the leadership of many of our corporate citizens is, to me, despicable. Are these corporate capitalists truly reflective of what the authors of capitalism had in mind?

Many of those who scream the loudest in defense of what they view as capitalism are also amongst the staunchest defenders of things like the *Constitution of the United States of America*.

"This is what our founding fathers had in mind," they cry out! Or "This course of action most certainly would not have been approved by our founding fathers!"

they bellow. All the while, they are ever mindful, that those same creators of our time-honored manuscript were being guided by the hand of DIVINE imperative. If the gold standard, ought to be that which was original as to intention and action, one should apply that same methodology and attitude, toward what the originators of the doctrine of capitalism had in mind.

Why is this important? Why should it merit being the focus of this next-to-last leg of our journey? Because we need to be aligned with the moral essence of the CREATOR, whether it be from a perspective of a loving relationship, or an inviolable decree of the universe. "As you sow, so shall you reap" and "what goes around comes around," are not just nice sayings. They contain truth. Karma is unavoidable. Given these truths, this topic is vitally important.

It has been suggested that capitalism, in its simplest form, is a type of economic system, characterized by private ownership of property, which is then used to generate a private profit. It is not a social or political system. That being said, permit me to present the notion that GOD intends for DIVINE CREATION to be free - free from tyranny, oppression, persecution, restricted transport or opportunity, free from injury or destruction to property or person. If we live in a democracy, we willingly cede a meaningful portion of these freedoms to our governments, for the expected common and self-serving good for all (or so we think). There is no such thing as capitalism in any pure, unadulterated form. I repeat. Capitalism, in its purest sense, does not exist. To believe, otherwise, is fantasy. To consider for a moment, that any elected official, would be capable of producing capitalism in some uncontaminated mode, is a flight of the imagination. Their claims of such are always revealed as patently disingenuous once elected.

What we do have is consensual capitalism by the majority. There are, in the United States and in other nations of the world, democratically elected governments that are given the powers to enact and enforce laws that are supposed to reflect the will of the people that elected them. In practice, our elected officials should model our standards, our priorities, and values. They should reflect how we wish to see capitalism defined and exercised. In view of this impact on each and every one of us, each citizen of every democracy has a duty, a sacred responsibility, to choose to take the quality of time required to investigate, so they can really learn where each of their would-be officials stand, on the issues that are most important to them. This should include their views on the free market system and, what the implications of such positions and policies would be to them individually, and to society as a whole.

Forget about what is said on the campaign trail to gain votes from their constituency. What has their <u>history</u> been, whether it is in the private or public sector? Introduce this into the equation. Should effective capitalism, worth standing for and endorsing, be subject to a moral code? If so, how and who defines that code? I personally wish that mankind, whether individuals or business entities, would consistently choose to have a heart for all of DIVINE CREATION. I would like to see freedom from excessive governmental oversight and regulation (other than the protection of person and property), and where capitalism would make a valuable difference wherever and whenever the needs arose. This would be a capitalistic utopia. Can you imagine? A world with no bureaucratic barriers to the creation and accumulation of wealth, partnered with a laser-like focus to continually make life-changing differences according to one's passions and callings.

I truly wish this could be so. Imagine a world where our lives are intertwined, so enmeshed, and in harmony with intended DIVINE DESIGN, that personal opulence, avarice and greed would be unimaginable. This would truly create "heaven on earth." I fear that this is a picture of a world yet to come. They are the fancies of a hopeless romantic, the predilections of a dreamer, and the longings for what can and should be.

Now that we have defined the "ideal" world, we must look at the "real" world. Our world society is a mixed bag. It contains everything from the furthest extremities of self-indulgence, ego and hedonism - to selflessness, self-denial, selling out and everything in-between. We live in a world of marginal to widespread bureaucratic intervention. All of the bureaucrats have varying levels of inefficiency, irresponsibility, personal agenda, power brokering, deceit, half-truths and corruption.

Is the answer to personal and corporate decadence and reckless abandon, government malfeasance and sleaze? I believe it is simply a case of "the blind leading the blind." There is decadence and reckless abandon, hidden behind the rhetoric of all political parties' ideologies and agendas. Given the realities of our world as mentioned above, is this just a zero sum game?

Does bureaucratic intervention, in all of its various forms, result in any meaningful and substantive difference for good? Clearly, the more intrusive the role of government, the further from pure capitalism we find ourselves drifting. Throughout history, the best efforts of government to right the perceived inequalities of society, was to provide bandages for some, but left most still wanting. All came to eventually see the sheer folly of the answers provided by their government, as these solutions eventually bled out - because they were never cures. All the bandages have ever done is cover up and mask the disease. It is very clear. If the governments were paying attention, the effective and loving answers would not be found in handouts without cost or sacrifice. This type of response only empowers weakness, making the weak even weaker. Instead, we should all be taught how to fish for ourselves.

This theory runs in the face of governments, because all have one thing in common: the need to feel needed. How do we, as a society, break free from the clutches of this self-serving, misguided, delusional and paternalistic agenda, and move toward self-determination and freedom? How do we rid ourselves, as a society, from our owners? These controllers regularly sell us on the notion that we are free, while passing laws and regulations that advocate and promote control, corruption, ravenous monetary consumption, bondage and worse.

In sum, how do we, the people, counteract the voracious, predatory and persistent onslaught of government everywhere, from becoming our uninvited landlord or our sugar daddy with counterfeit benevolence? Whatever became of a government "of the people, by the people and for the people?" To be candid, if we are ever going to experience capitalism in as pure a form as is reasonably possible and practical, it is going to be up to "the people" – every single one of us.

CAPITALISM OF THE PEOPLE, BY THE PEOPLE AND FOR THE PEOPLE

For true capitalism and freedom to have a bright and lasting future, entrepreneurs everywhere, are going to have to adopt a dramatic new paradigm - a model that acknowledges and responds to the needs of those less fortunate, by first meeting the requirements of their daily bread. There needs to be a shift, to investing in effective resources that will allow realistic opportunities to those less fortunate. There needs to be the possibility for not only climbing out of their dismal holes, but also becoming entrepreneurs and mentors themselves. This is going to require an acknowledgement, that there exists a DIVINE imperative to meet the needs of those who are experiencing poverty, hardship and destitution. Either we, the people, will meet these needs, or government will provide legislation for us, in the form of ever-burdensome rules and regulations.

One way or another, the immediate needs of the worlds' less fortunate must be met. Their cries will not go unheard forever, as these voices represent votes, and votes translate into re-election and ongoing power. Morality aside, which approach would you prefer? 1)The essentials of many being met by the creative, progressive and entrepreneurial abilities of businessmen and women everywhere or, 2) the oppressive hand of government, as it exacts its mandates upon its citizens, who oftentimes focus on its entrepreneurial community, in the form of burdensome taxation and life-choking rules and regulations? I know what my answer is. At the end of the day, there are only two results.

One, there is the inexpressible and inexplicable joy that comes from making a life-changing investment in others. Two, there is the option of continuing down the same old road of wanton self-indulgence and excess, where the government will impose its own form of morality, balance and redistribution upon the people. There will be no joy associated with this form of aid, only resentment.

On a smaller scale, but a no less meaningful one, I was greatly encouraged, as well as challenged recently, as I was talking with a blessed friend on the telephone. He advised me, that he and his two children had sponsored a needy family prior to a celebrated holiday season, and were about to go shopping for them. My esteemed and benevolent friend and his children would ensure, through their own personal generosity, that the holiday season for this family in need, would be different. They had the means and power to make it happen, and they did. From the sumptuous dinner, to the carefully thought out and researched presents for each family member, nothing was lacking. My friends required no one and nothing to motivate them. This was not the invention of a government plan for redistribution, nor was it motivated by any seed of guilt. Simply, quietly and without fanfare or celebrity, my friend and his children changed reality for a needy family, and in doing so, demonstrated that capitalism of the heart works!

What were the benefits of this action? Who can know the ripple effect that may have been started by this act? How it might powerfully play itself out? How many more lives might be touched to do the same and even greater? Might it become a global movement? While the answers to these questions remain unanswered and are yet to be discovered, one thing remains certain - the value of the legacy my friend has shown and left forever with his children, is beyond measure.

What of the impact on the family in need? What is preferred? A handout from a government that breeds a spirit of entitlement, while enabling weakness and fostering an environment of dependency? This chokes off personal potential, achievement and the glory associated with these accomplishments. What does it feel like to be the recipient of an act of private capitalism, with true philanthropy at its core and requires no repayment? There is a profound sense of personal significance and joy one experiences, when choosing to invest in and make a difference in the lives of others. This action might make the greatest difference on the recipient families' future; might make an enduring statement in the hearts of the children; may create hope and inspire everyone involved to stretch further, dream bigger, hold on longer and commit more fully.

In very clear terms, we who have been blessed (that includes you and everyone who has ever taken this walk with me), are really the authors of what form of capitalism we will pass on to our children, our world, and to future generations.

I would like to invite you to simply reflect on this matter of government entitlement vs. private individual philanthropy in its many and diverse forms. Think of an act of compassion that proactively reaches out to meet the needs of all of GOD's creation and lights a fire within you. I am curious and excited to hear what your thoughts are. Get a good rest, for we are about to begin the home stretch of our walk together. In many ways, what I will be sharing with you ahead, represents the most awesome change I have ever encountered and been challenged by! I even considered giving up on my personal and professional visions. It might have been the most daunting obstacle I have ever encountered, and has also become my greatest triumph.

Rest Stop

THE WALK®

CHAPTER 6

FAITH - WHATEVER YOU FOCUS ON GETS LARGER

Hoping for the best; getting what you expect.

Let's get finished! Actually, this glorious walk never truly arrives and does not stop. Our lives should be a never-ending journey, an enduring quest. This raises the most important question I will pose to you during this walk. Are you ready to endure?

Are you resolutely dedicated, committed to pressing on towards the achievement of gaining your highest - that which opens the door to your inheritance and your abundance, no matter what obstacles life presents to you? No matter how bleak the circumstances are, how dark the night, how truly overwhelming and insurmountable the obstacles may appear, are you ready to continue?

I suppose one can never truly know the answer to this question, until one is confronted with the apparent obstructions that separate one from victory.

I wish I could tell you that life and the eventual attainment of the prize is linear, that there are not moments that will cause you to question whether it is all worthwhile, and that there will not be times that you're emotional and physical bank accounts are nearing empty. I need to tell you that there will be such times, even to the point of being overdrawn. There will be moments where simply taking another breath, seems to take all the strength you can muster. It is here, in the eye of the storm, that you must discover the way forward. It is here, that you must unearth the courage and call upon your most effective resources, to face whatever stands between you, and your personal and finest triumphs.

Why am I calling on you to be so determined, so steadfast, so tenacious at the bleakest moment? It is because at that very instant, when you are closer than you ever have been to achieving your breakthrough – that you are ready to create your very own "heaven on earth." Success lies just beyond the veil. Trust me - you can breach the chasm. It is just there on the other side of the curtain. You must dig deep within yourself, and call upon that last ounce of strength. It is at the very second that you feel you are completely drained, that you will discover you are not! Somehow there is a bit more, a reserve you did not know existed. This is your final trial, and with it, the vision for your biggest future. Will it all be worth it? More than words can express, but please allow me to try.

It has been said, that whatever we focus on becomes larger, whether positive or negative. Reflect on the positive and we draw positive people, circumstances and results to our lives. Reflect on the negative and we reap precisely the opposite of all that we desire and need. So is this a magic bullet, a pathway and a shortcut to one's personal nirvana on the cheap and without cost? This popular mantra can be more destructive to its followers than the good it purports to offer. However, as I stated before, the road that leads to eventual, certain success and victory is not without potholes. At times, they will appear out of nowhere. They may have the appearance of being virtually insurmountable. Remember, however - appearances can be deceiving!

My own journey reflects one word: change. It embraces a belief system that always questions, always challenges, always remains open to...change. Not change for the sake of change, but an attitude that perhaps there is more to what I embrace, believe to be inviolate, perhaps an entirely different viewpoint,. An example would be my posture on matters of religion and faith. At one time I thought I had all the answers. Now, I have many more questions than answers. They are my questions and answers, not anyone else's. I cannot prove them nor do I feel the need to do so. I believe this is called FAITH.

I have been a student and follower of the "positive" for years, including being a voracious reader of outstanding literary works, all designed to transform the reader (me) in multiple, ever-growing and positive ways. I have had the great joy and privilege of reaching out and sharing with others during walks like this one. I have been so fortunate to gain from the wisdom of the ages so that others, too, might prosper and be an agent of positive change in the world. The expression, "Be careful what you wish for, because you just might get it" is so true. I "got it," in ways I could never have planned for or imagined.

It was just another Thursday morning, or so I thought. My wife and I began the day like thousands before it. We bathed, got dressed and headed for the breakfast table, where we would routinely discuss matters of interest, telephone family or friends, and address areas of timely importance. I can see myself sitting at the table, casually eating my breakfast as the phone rang. I answered it, wondering who it might be at such an early hour. I speculated as to the caller and what their message might be, but never, never could I have been prepared for the bomb that was about to fall. The caller on the other end of the line and what she had to say to me instantly turned my placid and composed morning into a virtual nightmare. It caused a shock so deep, I was sent into a state of near total disarray, confusion, fear, and anger. I felt such an all-consuming and abject sense, that, in an instant, I had become fully enveloped and consumed by darkness. It felt like I would never to see the light of day again.

Surely my biggest future as I had envisioned it, was now a mere pipe dream. All of the readings, reflections and best efforts I had invested countless hours in, all the focus on personal and powerful changes were now up in smoke. I felt powerless, vulnerable, defeated. I was done, or so I thought!

✡ ✡ ✡

IT IS WHEN I AM AT MY WEAKEST POINT, THAT I AM TRULY MY STRONGEST!

"You simply must first experience loss, to know true victory."

I had read the words attributed to Saul of Tarsus, and heard numerous renderings of *The New Testament's* passage on any number of occasions. They would have remained lifeless and impersonal to me, unless I experienced that fateful Thursday morning, and all that followed.

To put this situation in context, for the previous seven years leading up to that morning, I was the owner of a small but successful, growing company. I relied heavily on my administrative assistant (we will call her Catherine, not her real name), to supply a vast array of critically important services, from the administrative to working with clients, and a myriad number of duties in between. Our staff numbered two. She was one of the two, and you can guess who the other one was! Essentially I had fired myself from everything Catherine had been doing for years, so I could focus solely on my

"Unique Ability®." If something happened to her, through death, disability or sickness, our ability to function as a healthy, responsive enterprise, would initially be severely hampered.

In addition, two months prior to that morning, we had entered into an agreement to move out of our offices of seven years, which was a daunting undertaking, to say the least! The move was to have occurred one week later from that particular morning, and nothing had been packed: not the files, books, computers and printers, the piles of stuff we had amassed over the years. Catherine was going to do the packing the following week. It is a moot point whether we should have been in that position one week before a major move. It simply had not been done and that was that. Our ability to make the move to our new office, which we were now under contract to fulfill, would be severely hampered, should something happen to Catherine.

Prior to this morning, I had negotiated a major change in our professional company affiliations, which included the opening of a second office location situated about two hours away. The grand opening was scheduled for ten days later. A volume of administrative and paper-intensive complexity was involved. If piled one document upon another, it would resemble the harvesting of a great number of trees. This administrative nightmare (and I am not overstating the nature of this transition) was one that, under ideal conditions, would have taken at least three months to complete. If it were not completed, it would have resulted in the permanent loss of thousands of dollars. Far worse, it could have rendered our small, regular cash flow-dependent enterprise, insolvent. Our ability to make this transition on a timely basis was paramount to continuing to receive our cash flow, to say nothing of opening our new office location.

I had been asking and praying for real and substantive change in my life on multiple levels for years. I received it all, or so it seemed, on that one particular morning. My administrative assistant, the right hand to my left hand, had been in a horrific motorcycle accident the evening before, and would be incapacitated for several months or longer. In an instant, I was a company of <u>one</u>.

While I was sitting at the table (hunched over is more accurate) in abject despondency and resigned to my apparent fate, an angel appeared. Angels can take many forms, and appear when you least expect them. It is true that, "The temptations (*tests*) in your life are no different from what others experience. And GOD is faithful. HE will not allow the temptation *(test)* to be more than you can stand. When you are tempted *(tested)*, HE will show you a way out so you can endure." (1 Corinthians 10:13; *New Living Translation of the HOLY BIBLE).*

The angel in this case, was my wife Fran. I was completely focused on failure, on what we were lacking and our distressing predicament. I was playing the role of victim. My attention was on the material world - that which can be seen and is limited. Fran was focused on what we could control, and what incremental progress we could make, which would lead us to victory. She was intent on succeeding on purpose! Her single-mindedness was of the spiritual realm – that which is unseen and has no limits.

"Let's get to the office and start packing," she said. "We'll be just fine." Her calm, steadfast and assuring demeanor was salve to my spirit. It both soothed and calmed my fears and anxiety, as quickly as they had appeared. It created the environment I needed to get re-energized, so that my thoughts and emotions were in alignment with Fran's, and with my own core belief system.

We deliberately focused on controlling all that we could, from that moment on - period. Our goals were set - from packing up the office in preparation for the move, soliciting some much needed help from a generous client who lived nearby, asking for a healthy dose of grace from the financial services firm we had just resigned from, to the actual move and the process of discovering our next administrative support person. What was the net result?

- The move to the new office took place right on time and went without a hitch.

- The cash flow of the business was unimpeded.

- We successfully opened our second office location as scheduled.

- The transition to the new financial services company was successfully completed.

- We hired a new administrative assistant that has a bright future with our company.

- A quantum number of new exciting relationships and resources has come across my path, resulting in a host of unintended and unplanned for blessings.

- I have made meaningful and quantifiable progress on multiple levels in my life - personally, professionally, and spiritually. I believe we are just getting started and that miraculous successes lie ahead.

What if I had given up? What if I had taken the path of least resistance? What if I had given into the darkness of the moment? What if I had not heard and responded positively to Fran's sage and timely counsel?

Clearly, the vision I said I so passionately desired would have gone up in smoke, and the journey I am now on, would have been only a pipe dream.

Do *you* want to experience change in *your* life? I do not mean incremental, finite change. I am referring to a dramatic transformation that results in your experiencing a personal_revolution, a major change in ideas and/or practice on multiple levels for your highest good-permanently. By extension, you will be impacting the world for the better perpetually as well, a global revolution by the same definition.

As you can tell from my experience, be assured that the earnestness and depth of your desire for personal change will, at times, be met with an equally determined, robust but inferior force, which will use whatever means are necessary and available to throw you off track, to abort you inheriting *the key* to your highest future. Be aware and mindful of this, so when it appears, you can say, "Aha! I have been expecting you!" Learn from what I have just shared from my own experience. Greet this resistance, as a confirmation of the progress you have made up to that point. It is a testament, to the reality that you are now much closer to the next leg of your journey, than you have ever been! I want you to understand this.

Just as I received (at precisely the right time) exactly what I needed, the GIVER OF ALL GOOD THINGS will bestow upon you all that you require, to overcome whatever apparent roadblock seems to be thwarting your quest at that moment. Your FAITH, if you stand resolute, will overcome anything that tries to stand in your way. GOD guarantees it!

You and I are close to the home stretch. This would be a good time to take a well-deserved, much-needed rest before we head back, as there is one more theme we still need to contemplate, before our walk together concludes for this time. For now, I would like to invite you to reflect on a few questions.

As you reflect back historically, is there anything whatsoever that you thought you deeply desired, but when resistance presented itself, your desire gradually waned under its weight? Your desire was most likely replaced by an acceptance that it just was not meant to be, the price was too high, the timing was just not right, or you thought of an endless variety of other excuses, for not seeing your dream through to its fulfillment. This leads to another important question to ask yourself. Is there anything in your present that is opposing you from making progress, toward something that you greatly aspire to?

Keeping in mind what I have just shared, and the absolute fact that defeat is never the friend of personal confidence, what strategy might you now consider? Is it time to revisit a former longing, or a current one, but with a new resolve, power and attitude. Again, as you reflect, please take all the time you require.

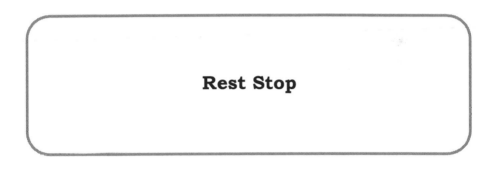

Rest Stop

THE WALK ®

CHAPTER 7

FAITH and REVOLUTION

**A call to personal and dramatic
change in ideas and practices.**

As we head on the final portion of our walk back home, I would like to conclude our present time together by focusing on one word: revolution. This word has profound and positive implications on our world and its inhabitants historically, and in our current affairs.

Let me tell you what I do not mean. I am not talking about a willful disobedience of the law, and a series of actions that violate the rights of others. I am not talking about revolution for revolutions sake. I am speaking about purpose-driven revolution. The reasons behind the plans and actions of purpose-filled revolution are what is important. The reasons are what give meaning and significance to the participants.

Revolution is not something new to our world, and should not be feared or avoided. To stop revolution from achieving the objectives once the time has ripened would be an enormous mistake. Though many have tried before, they have always been unsuccessful. A partial list will serve to make my point. The United States, still a young nation in global terms, has undergone the following revolutions with positive end results:

- The American Revolution, during the last half of the 18th century, resulted in the 13 North American colonies breaking away from the British Empire, which ruled it from overseas and without representation. This revolution led to the eventual formation of The United States of America. Verdict? A great thing!

- The Agricultural Revolution, from the 18th century to the end of the 19th century, saw a massive and rapid increase in agricultural productivity, and vast improvements in farm technology. Wages were high by global standards. It was not uncommon, for a person to work in the textile mills for a few years, save up enough money to purchase land and create his/her own business. The plows, seed drills, machines that harvest to this day, all owe their creation and improvement to The Agricultural Revolution. Verdict? A great thing!

- The Industrial Revolution, from the 18th to the 19th century, increased the living standards for the masses of ordinary people like never before. Changes in agriculture, manufacturing, mining, transportation and technology. All these transformations profoundly impacted mankind. Verdict? A great thing!

- The Women's Suffrage Movement (a revolution), began with one main goal: to achieve voting rights for women, by means of an amendment to the *Constitution of the United States of America.* It was finally realized on August 26, 1820. Verdict? A great thing!

- The passage of the 13th Amendment to the *Constitution of the United States of America*, ratified on December 6, 1865, effectively abolished slavery in the United States (a revolution) and provided that, "Neither slavery nor involuntary servitude, except as a punishment for crime whereof, the party shall have been duly convicted, shall exist within the United States, or any place subject to their jurisdiction." Verdict? A great thing!

- The Technological Revolution? What used to take weeks by mail, now takes fractions of seconds via the Internet. In the developed world, the Internet has ushered in the greatest period of wealth-creation in history. It has undermined and disrupted traditional power structures, and changed the way industry and the world conducts business. The Austrian economist, Joseph Schumpeter, coined the term *"Creative Destruction,"* which denotes "a process of industrial mutation that incessantly revolutionizes the economic structure from within, incessantly destroying the old one, incessantly creating a new one." The proverbial cat is out of the bag, and will not be getting back in. Technology is lightning fast and getting faster. Change is here to stay. So when did the Technological Revolution begin? It might be reasonably argued, that the commercial introduction of the microchip vs. the transistor, ushered in the revolution, in which case 1961 would be the start date. Verdict? An amazing thing!

- The American Gay Rights Revolution, spawned from 1924 to the present, began with the creation of *The Society for Human Rights* (the earliest known gay rights organization). Then, in 1956, the founding of

The Daughters of Bilitis, pioneered a national lesbian organization. Illinois began decriminalizing same-sex intercourse between consenting adults (done in private) in 1962. The American Psychiatric Association removed homosexuality from its official list of mental disorders, in 1973. The implementation of *"Don't Ask, Don't Tell"* in 1993, led Vermont to become the first state to recognize same-sex civil unions in 2000, and went on to become the first state recognizing same-sex marriage on April 7, 2009. A litany of progress follows. Verdict? A great thing!

• Recently, we have had Occupy Wall Street, a leaderless global movement and most definitely, a revolution. It began in 2011, and will continue until who knows when? Do I agree with everything that is being espoused by the millions of people who are a part of this movement? Absolutely not! Do I clearly understand the abject frustration of many of its adherents? Without a doubt! If you want to know who the true authors of this revolution really are, you can easily identify them. They are the financially fortunate ones, who have turned a blind eye to poverty, to abuse in all its ugly forms, to once-proud homeowners, now living in the streets and to the inner city breadlines. Many in positions of power have corrupted the public trust. These people are the blame-shifters, who fostered and passed policy that was destined for the recent U.S. meltdown, widespread misery, and general degradation of American society. Still today, their unrestrained debauchery continues. It will not last much longer.

I wish I could honestly say that those entrepreneurs who have amassed great financial wealth, that have been fortunate enough, by DIVINE GRACE, to gain not only financial wealth, but also power and influence, will do the <u>right thing</u>. I wish I could say that they will choose to open their hearts, their eyes and their wallets, to the suffering that is going on all over the world, and in their own backyards. Yet, I do not believe the majority of the wealthy are willing to do so. They are too busy blaming those less fortunate, and those affected by the current status of the economy, for the predicaments they find themselves in. They refer to the affected 99% of our country that have been financially challenged, as losers, lazy, trash and rabble-rousers. They continue to point the finger at others. It is much easier for the other 1% (the super- rich), to do that than to take an honest look at their own lives. Why? Because they would have to change the entire way they live! They would have to put off buying that new toy, the next cruise, that diamond ring, the bigger home, and subordinating their insatiable appetite for <u>more</u>. The bottom line is the wealthy would have to admit to their greed.

What does all this have to do with FAITH? Plenty! Am I advocating a widespread government-mandated redistribution of wealth, from the haves to the have-nots? A system, where those that sacrifice to achieve more, share the spoils with those that have chosen to live off the hard work of others? No! Absolutely not!

What I am encouraging, supporting, even pleading for, is a personal and widespread fundamental change in how everyone views the world, its inhabitants, treasures, and the stewardship of it all. I am pledging that we were called by the DIVINE from the very beginning. I am endorsing a way of living that sees beyond immediate personal gratification, and chooses to see and embrace the struggles of others less fortunate. To aid and provide to these human beings an effective, long-term way out of their plight, whether financial, emotional, educational, physical, or a combination of all. I am validating a world system that truly provides equal opportunity, for everyone to achieve his or her highest potential on multiple levels. I am asking for a world and the environment that does not tread on the necks and backs of others, but one that supports, encourages and celebrates their successes. We need a world, not of competition and limited thinking, but one of creativity with no limits whatsoever. We can no longer tolerate a world of veiled secrecy and cover-ups. We need total transparency. This entire planet, requires a kinder, more honest, sensitive, and respectful path of living. Our world systems are broken: economically, politically, environmentally, sociologically, and morally. It is all in tatters.

WE NEED A REVOLUTION - AND
THE REVOLUTION IS YOU!

Make no mistake about it. Should you feel like I do, there will be no shortage of people and institutions that will oppose you, will go to great lengths to undermine you and your passion, and will brand you a nut case. You will be considered a person unworthy of time or attention. And then, the greater their fervor against you, the closer you are getting to hitting their hot button, upsetting their apple cart, and getting to the bottom line truth about them, and that which they are protecting. You are getting dangerously close to that which they cherish and worship - the god of capitalism. Yes, capitalism (and its meaning) has changed over the years. As we discussed before, it is now defined by one's political bias and approach to economics. What is truly fascinating is the fact that the ascribed father of capitalism, would find disfavor among the extreme right today. He would even be branded a socialist at the least, a communist at the worst.

Arguably, the acknowledged father of both capitalism and economics was Adam Smith, the author of *Wealth of Nations*. Mr. Smith foresaw a system, "where whole economies profited and not the privileged few." He promoted a system known as monopoly capitalism in its extreme, wherein there are fewer sellers of things and many more buyers.

It is my theory, that if we continue down this road of greed, wanton accumulation and avarice by the few, we will eventually have a monopsony (a system where there are many sellers of things and fewer buyers), and an economic tsunami with no winners. Smith also discredited, as patently ineffective, any system which tended to protect individual producers. For example, the present-day mantra of the political right is that raising taxes on the mega-wealthy is anathema. In fact, Smith said, "The rich should contribute . . . not in proportion to their revenue, but something more than that in proportion." If Adam Smith were alive today and was to repeat the above, I believe it is clear how he would be branded by the so-called conservative movement of our day. How things have changed.

But never mind what Adam Smith had to say about foundational capitalism. What about Jesus of Nazareth (no matter what or who you believe him to be - rabbi, teacher, prophet, Son of the Most High)? What are some of the things HE had to say, when it came to matters of money, property, stewardship, government, taxes, wealth accumulation, and our fellow earthly sojourners?

WAS JESUS PROPOSING A REVOLUTION? TO BE SURE, HE WAS THE REVOLUTIONIST OF ALL REVOLUTIONISTS!

* "Then Jesus said to them, 'Watch out! Be on your guard against all forms of greed; a man's life does not consist in the abundance of his possessions." Luke 12:15

* "No one can serve two masters. Either he will hate the one and love the other, or he will be devoted to the one and despise the other. You cannot serve both God and Money." Matthew 6:24

* "For I was hungry and you gave me nothing to eat, I was thirsty and you gave me nothing to drink, I was a stranger and you did not invite me in, I needed clothes and you did not clothe me, I was sick and in prison and you did not look after me." They will also answer, "Lord, when did we see you hungry or thirsty or a stranger or needing clothes or sick or in prison, and did not help you?" He will reply, "I tell you the truth, *whatever you did not do for one of the least among you, you did not do for me.*" Matthew 25:42-45.

* "Command those who are rich in this present world not to be arrogant nor to put their hope in wealth, which

149

is so uncertain, but to put their hope in God, who richly provides us with everything for our enjoyment. Command them to do good, to be rich in good deeds, and to be generous and willing to share." 1 Timothy 6:17-18.

• "After Jesus and his disciples arrived in Capernaum, the collectors of the two-drachma tax came to Peter and asked, "Does not your teacher pay the temple tax?" "Yes, he does," he replied. When Peter came into the house, Jesus was the first to speak. 'What do you think, Simon? he asked. From whom do the kings of the earth collect duty and taxes - from their own sons or from others?" "From others," Peter answered. "Then the sons are exempt, Jesus said to him. But so that we may not offend them, go to the lake and throw out your line. Take the first fish you catch; open its mouth and you will find a four-drachma coin. Take it and give it to them for my tax and yours." Matthew 17:24-27.

WOW! If that is not the voice of revolution, then I do not know what is.

How can millions (not all for sure) of so-called Jesus followers, be so indifferent to these and so many other things HE said, that plead the cases of the downtrodden, the abused, the least among us? Could it be that they are being misled by the god of modern day capitalism, the one who is the deceiver of many, including the so-called faithful?

What did Mohammed have to say to the people of his day and to his devotees today? As to matters of contentment, Mohammed said all of the following:

• "Riches are not from an abundance of worldly goods, but from a contented mind."

• "Look to those inferior to yourselves, so that you may not hold God's benefits in contempt."

• "When you see a person who has been given more than you in money and beauty, then look to those who have been given less."

When it came to monopolies, Mohammed said all of the following:

• "The holder of a monopoly is a sinner and an offender."

• "The bringers of grain to the city to sell at a cheap rate gain immense advantage by it, and those who keep back grain in order to sell at a high rate are cursed."

The barriers that have been constructed in our societies today, are in multi-layered forms, and are designed to keep the other guy down and in his place. These must be taken down, so everyone can have their chance to realize their dreams.

Am I advocating that those in positions of power and wealth willingly cede their good fortune? Not at all! Am I promoting that they abandon the iron-fisted grip they have on controlling and defending the entry points to equal opportunity for all? You bet I am!

I am suggesting that we promote and celebrate the creative universe where there is plenty for all to have and to enjoy, according to their hearts" desire. Not a competitive world, where there are a few winners and many losers. Interestingly, this revolution I envision, unbeknownst to the powerbrokers at this time, benefits them as well. I am simply advocating a system, where all people have access to the same opportunities, and where all the barriers to advancement by the masses are torn down.

Can we realistically expect those that line up behind the model of modern day capitalism, to buy into what I am encouraging? For most of them, the answer is no!

This is why our current reality suggests, that we do need the resources of government to partner with us, if we are to provide any sort of a level playing field. We, the people, need those elected "by and for us", to help bring about a societal reset. This would provide an environment which promotes the legislation, monetary means and resources, to recognize, validate, encourage and finance the creativity and hard work of others. This would then allow the yet-undiscovered creativity of each person, to become unearthed from within and to grow. We require an atmosphere, where entire economies and societies are the beneficiaries. No longer can we uphold the privileged few. We must now have a capitalism of the people, by the people and for the people. This is capitalism that the DIVINE can endorse.

THIS IS FAITH-BASED CAPITALISM!

We are almost at the end of this walk together. We have addressed and reflected carefully, on a number of extremely volatile and passionate themes in our world today.

Before we head back, it's time for one last rest. It's time to reflect on this chapter's hotly debated subjects. This is an opportunity, in light of what I have just shared, to have the courage to ask yourself where you stand on these matters, and to find a very personal response. Remember, the way in which we individually and collectively define these issues going forward, will impact everyone on the planet for all time to come.

Rest Stop.

✡ ✡ ✡

THE WALK®

CHAPTER 8

HEADING FOR HOME
The Starting Point for the Rest of Your Life.

"God is a circle whose center is everywhere
and whose circumference is nowhere."
Anonymous. *The Book of the Twenty-Four
Philosophers (12ᵗʰ Century)*

Now that you have had time to carefully reflect on this final theme during our walk, I have some things I want to share with you as we head for the finish line. When I say finish line, I mean to suggest that in only one way: It's the end of our walk for <u>now</u>! I trust that we will be walking together on different occasions in the future, and in different ways. Sometimes, it will be just you and me. At other times, we will walk with others who are on their own journeys. Both venues, will offer the opportunity for powerful new insights, self-discovery and empowerment.

By the way, did it occur to you, that since we started our walk together, that we have been walking in a circle? That was very deliberate on my part. The entire universe has been fashioned by the CREATOR to operate on a circular principal. The circle is a representation of the infinite nature of energy, and the inclusivity of the universe. Think about it. *The Torah* says, that mankind was created from the dust of the earth, and to the earth, as dust, mankind shall return. The sun's grand entrance every morning becomes its evening farewell, and says with assurance, "I will greet you again in the morning." Our four seasons go from one to the next, forever repeating the cycle. A wild animal eats a subordinate animal for its food. After a while, the wild animal passes away, and the nutrients in its body enter the soil, to be consumed by another subordinate animal, for its food. Eventually, it too is consumed, continuing the cycle of life. The planets are circular, and they too inexorably revolve around the sun, in circular fashion. The numbers of illustrations I could cite to make the point are without limit.

Now please listen carefully. Listen deeply. The reliability of the cycle of life hinges on one word: balance. The very future of our planet and all of its inhabitant, is dependent on a fragile, delicate and ordered balance. We have now become a world that is so off-center, so lopsided, and out of kilter, that it is just a matter of time before we reach a tipping point. It will be a point of no return.

What keeps the earth reliably in orbit around the sun and from not being jettisoned in a straight line, out into the depths of space? What enables an aircraft with people and other objects on board to takeoff, climb, cruise, descend and land without incident? What ensures that there will always be plenty of available food to meet all living creatures' daily requirements? What principle is in play that enables us to work at our jobs or careers, giving all we have to give every day and yet, able to return the next day to do it over and over again? The answer in each case is balance.

We have talked about, and carefully reflected upon a number of crucially important matters of our day. These are topics that are deeply impassioned, and sometimes forcefully divide, rather than unite. These matters seemingly bring us perilously close to the edge of the abyss, time and time again. We are playing chicken with the DIVINE, if you will. It appears as if no real substantive change can occur without first experiencing, a tectonic shift. I am not speaking of the forces or conditions that impact the earth's crust as in an earthquake, but a force that is even more potent and more powerful.

I am referring to a tectonic shift of the heart. These shifts are inescapable, relentless forces that impact and compel us; that move and change our thoughts, priorities, values, decisions, passions, and create our very own personal revolution. Our world desperately needs such a dramatic transformation. The times of bandage solutions are long past. Mankind's so-called conventional thinking, with all of the personal agendas behind the human intellect, has been tried without succeeding. It has been found, in the court of universal jurisdiction, to be ineffective, faulty and not whole. Enough is enough! It is time for change. We need a change that flows from the very heart and mind of the DIVINE, GOD.

How do we personally experience this life-changing moment, this altered state? Is this something your physician can prescribe? Can you buy it over the counter? Can you reason or intellectualize yourself there? Can you catch it from someone else, like a cold? Is this something you can study for, and then write a qualifying exam to attain? Will you receive it through regular attendance at a church, a synagogue, a mosque, a temple? To all of the above, the answer is NO!

This awareness is not something that is attained cheaply. It is something you desire with all of your heart, for as long as it takes. You can be sure of this - heaven will visit you, if you persist. Your heart <u>will</u> be changed and this change <u>will</u> be an idyllic personal reset moment. It will be your own virtual Garden of Eden reclaimed. I see you are intrigued, and, hopefully, up to the task! So what is next?

I invite you to reflect back on all of the various themes we have discussed on our walk. Choose one, just one, which resonated within you as we were walking and during the rest stop experiences. I began our walk, talking about the crucial importance of knowing what specific destination you are heading for, by design. Did that connect with you? We then talked about the fact that, in life, as we head toward our inheritance - our highest and best - there is simply no free lunch. There are certain hurdles and challenges. When you heard that, how did it make you feel? Next, I presented you with a vision: the challenges will be 100% worth it, as you learn to see ahead of you, all the wealth of opportunities that arc waiting to be discovered. I trust that this insight energized you!

What about the reflections on all of the life experiences you have had, that should empower you with confidence? Was that a catalytic moment for you? Did you identify with the theme focused on faith, at a time when I, myself, thought I knew it all? Did **The Walk**® regarding matters of faith and life partners, with all of its relationship implications, connect with you? How about the deeply passionate topic on faith and the Gay, Lesbian, Bi-Sexual, Trans-Gender community? Did this deeply divisive thesis get your attention? Or did the ideas I expressed as to faith and politics strike a chord?

What about the arguments that I proffered regarding faith and capitalism? Did that evoke a heart response? People can have very strong opinions when it comes to that premise. One of my favorites is the notion that what we focus on, invariably gets larger, be it positive or negative. Did your ears perk up, when I addressed the issues related to that area? Finally, what about the focus on revolution, and the need for a tectonic shifting of our hearts? I cannot think of a more desperate plea on our part, for the DIVINE to visit and change us from the inside out.

Now that you have identified the one subject that spoke to you in the clearest voice, I am going to share with you something that should become as natural to you as breathing, a tool that will become a habit if you commit to it daily. It can transform your life for the better, permanently. It will change who you are, in ways that you could never have imagined. I am going to share, with you how to tap into the wisdom of the AGELESS ONE. I want you to become a great thinker.

I call it "900 Seconds. How the Next 15 Minutes Can Create the Abundant Future You Desire - Starting Now." Other people, who have plugged into this gem, have seen changes in their lives on multiple levels. It is one of those things, that departs from conventional thinking, primarily because it is so very simple. And here it is!

Conventional thinking goes something like this: REALLY BIG and REALLY IMPORTANT events and results, follow REALLY BIG plans, which consume REALLY BIG amounts of time, and involve REALLY BIG numbers of people, and cost REALLY BIG money.

Well, CONVENTIONAL THINKING IS WRONG!

One of the problems with conventional thinking is that it's rarely involved in the act and the art of **deeply focused, concentrated, and laser-like thought.** Oftentimes, another agenda trumps the earnest desire, for **real truth and real wisdom**. It becomes a matter, of putting <u>my</u> cart, before the other guy's horse. Every single time this happens, it *negates access to the very storehouse, the very essence of receiving powerful insight,* and **true wisdom. This wisdom of** mankind severs the cord which ties each and every one of us, to **the ALL-KNOWING**. It corrupts the very core of receiving, a **DIVINE DOWNLOAD**.

Another problem with conventional thought is in thinking that your biggest future, somehow resides in the actions, decisions and priorities of others. This includes any government and it involves bureaucrats everywhere, selling the notion that they are in the know. Then, they can control the masses in a multitude of ways, and seek to fulfill their own personal agendas. They can brainwash people into believing, that only they have the right answers for everyone.

This denigrates the very reality, as to how you were created. Everything was thought into existence by **the UNIVERSAL CREATIVE ONE**. All of existence is flawlessly linked to **the UNIVERSAL CREATIVE ONE**. Any attempt for total control, diminishes the creative geniuses of Thomas Edison, Alexander Graham Bell, George Westinghouse, Albert Einstein, Benjamin Franklin and, more recently, Steve Jobs. Well, I have GREAT NEWS for you: *YOU ARE THE NEXT EDISON, THE NEXT JOBS. BELIEVE IT*!

Yet another misinterpretation by conventional thought is that we live in a competitive universe. WRONG AGAIN! While it is true, that our world systems are based on competition, the universe is one of infinite capacity and creativity. The more we buy into a culture of competition, the more we will be drawn into being pawns for the agendas of others, and detracted from attaining our own highest and creative best. We are the greatness we were created to be. Creation was not meant to be a history of winners and losers, but an entire universe of winners! We are all designed to experience a personal first place, .*a world where everyone champions the passions and causes of each other.*

Finally, one last arrow in the bubble of conventional thought (although this rendering on conventional thinking is by no means complete). While there are glorious riches to be gleaned from the writings, the sayings, the experiences, the intellect of others, these should, in no way, be _a replacement for regularly investing in your own original thoughts_. You **must** develop *the art of self-thought*. Yes, this takes effort, it takes time, and it requires an act of the will. If there are glorious riches to be learned from the thoughts of others, *there are unfathomable and_unspeakable treasures yet to be unearthed, by you.* They have been waiting for you to mine them. Only you, can manifest these certain jewels into earthly existence. The truth is this: ***you** are a vessel* *for* **DIVINE** *creative expression.* You alone, will determine whether the world will be the beneficiary of the blessings that reside within you that are crying out to be born. ***The beginning of the rest of your life starts right now.***

Here is all you need and it's all free:

- a quiet sanctuary (any place where you won't be disturbed), which might include a favorite place for walking or light hiking (remember, no distractions whatsoever) and 15 minutes;

- a subject or object of your thoughts;

- a "beginner's mind" *which chooses to empty your mind of everything you think you know* as to the object or subject of your thinking;

- a looking within yourself as to **the SOURCE** of the wisdom;

- an act of the will to remain steadfastly focused on the object or subject *for the entire 15_minutes (this is a habit which develops and becomes easier with time);*

- the faith that you **WILL** be spoken to, and will receive true wisdom (either within the allotted 15 minutes or thereafter). *True wisdom is going to visit you;*

- once you receive what is uniquely for you, *you will act on it, once the allotted 15 minutes_are up;* and

- *you will make an appointment with yourself for 15 minutes* **every day,** *to practice the art of self-thought, and show up for the appointment without excuse.*

Make this a personal commitment. Make it a priority promise to yourself.

I would be honored if you would share the bounty you discover with me. This will be my joy-filled reward, for sharing my thoughts and heart with you on this walk. I will be cheering you on, as you attain your highest goals, your best in all things. <u>Do not ever settle for anything less. You and you alone, can determine what your future looks like: 15 minutes at a time!</u>

That is it.

You have graduated to your next level. Remember however, there are an infinite number of destinations on your journey. I am so very proud of you. You are one of a growing number of seekers worldwide, who feel a relentless pull towards the truth, and the wisdom that has long been hidden and suppressed. You are seeking a standard that defies mere human logic and reasoning.

Human ideals and principles no longer cut it with you. You want, and require, infinitely more. You yearn for a more dynamic relationship with the TRUE SOURCE, the INFINITE, and THE WAY. Soon, I will be inviting you to take another walk with me. A walk that will build on the experiences you have had on this walk, and the days that follow. Remember, do not <u>ever</u> allow others to steal from the unmistakable inner voice that is calling you to reach higher, to mine your heart more deeply. Many may scoff at you. But, do not judge them or react to them, for they are on their own path and cannot yet hear what you hear. They still answer to "the voice of men." Simply, do not empower their influence over you and your pathway.

My friend, we have come full circle. How time has flown by! I have enjoyed beyond words, the time we have spent together. I have been blessed because of you. I have equipped you with everything you need for now. I am already looking forward to next time!

I do not do farewells easily so allow me to just say: "I leave you for now with just two words that will most assuredly be the two most important words I could say at this moment

KEEP WALKING!"

✡ ✡ ✡

THE BEGINNING!

THE WALK®

SELECTED BIBLIOGRAPHY

Anonymous. 12th Century. *The Book of the Twenty-Four Philosophers.*

Aristotle (384 BC-322 BC). Quote: *"We are what we repeatedly do. Excellence therefore is not an act but a habit."*

Boorstin, Daniel J. (1914-2004). Paper entitled *Extreme Perspective.* Library of Congress. 1984.

Burke, Edmund (1729-1797). Quote: *"All that's necessary for the forces of evil to win in the world is for enough good men to do nothing."*

Carroll, Lewis. *Alice's Adventures in Wonderland.* London, UK: Macmillan and Co. Lewis, 1865.

Chapman, Gary D. *The 5 Love Languages: The Secret to Love That Lasts.* Chicago, IL. Northfield Publishing. 1992.

Cooper, Robert K., Ph.D. *Get Out Of Your Own Way - The 5 Keys to Surpassing Everyone's Expectations.* New York, USA: Crown Business, an imprint of The Crown Publishing Group, a Division of Random House, Inc. 2006.

Coyle, Daniel. *The Talent Code: Greatness Is Not Born. It is Grown. Here is How.* New York, NY: Bantam Dell, a Division of Random House, Inc. 2009.

Drucker, Peter F. Quote: *"Efficiency is doing things right; effectiveness is doing the right things."*

Hall, Kevin. *Aspire: Discovering Your Purpose through the Power of Words.* New York, NY, USA: Harper Collins Publishers. 2009.

Heath, Chip with Heath, Dan. *Made To Stick - Why Some Ideas Survive and Others Die.* New York, NY, USA: Random House, an imprint of The Random House Publishing Group, a Division of Random House, Inc. 2007.

Helminiak, Daniel A. *What the Bible Really Says About Homosexuality.* Tajique, NewMexico. Alamo Square Press. 2000.

Hoffer, Eric (1902-1983). Quote*: "In times of change, learners will inherit the Earth, while the knowers will find themselves beautifully equipped to deal with a world that no longer exists."*

Strategic Coach® and Unique Ability® are registered trademarks, protected by copyright and intellectual concepts of The Strategic Coach, Inc, all rights reserved. Used with written permission www.strategiccoach.com.

Scanzoni, Letha Dawson and Ramey Mollenkott. *Is the Homosexual My Neighbor? A Positive Christian Response.* New York NY: HarperCollins Publishers. 1978.

Schumpeter, Joseph (1883-1950). *Capitalism, Socialism and Democracy.* 1942.

Smith, Adam. *Wealth of Nations. Thrifty Books.* 2009

Stevens. Marsha J. For Those Tears I Died. Balm Publishing. 1993.

The Constitution of the United States of America. 13th Amendment. Ratified December 6, 1865.

The New International Version of The Bible. Published by Zondervan in the United States and by Hodder & Stoughton in the UK. Originally published in the 1970s, the *NIV* was most recently updated in 2011.

The New Testament.

The Torah.

THE WALK®

ABOUT THE AUTHOR

Alan Freedman has been a successful businessman and philanthropist both in Canada and the United States for over 44 years and is a lifelong student of life and life-change. He is a voracious reader and someone who is constantly challenging and questioning the authenticity of what he has held to be true as to any number of themes in life.

Alan Freedman and his wife, Fran - his best friend and life partner of 34 years and counting - have six children, (one gay), four grandchildren. They also have a household of six four-legged furry children, and are avid animal lovers, having co-founded Morning Starr Animal Sanctuary in 2001.

Alan moved to the United States from Toronto, Canada, 16 years ago. He is a man with an enormous heart and a human being whose enthusiasm for giving shows in a myriad of venues and ways. Alan comes to us with his vast experience from advising his financial and estate planning clients. Alan's clients are always also his friends. His passions are many:

Seeing legislation enacted to ensure dignity and preservation for all of GOD's animal creations. He is also an advocate for providing equality and meaningful resources for the gay, lesbian, bi-sexual and transgendered (GLBT) community on a global basis. He has a zeal for a specialized focus on the aging GLBT community, and the at-risk GLBT youth "on the street."

Alan promotes honest protection of all natural legacy treasures, to include a sound, sustainable policy toward our environment to reverse the erosion that has already begun. This achievement will showcase Capitalism as a system with a heart, that provides equal opportunity for everyone to become the highest and best that they can be. It will serve as a vehicle to provide a world view of abundance, where there are no losers, versus one of scarcity, where competition and greed predominates.

Creating legislation to protect our natural resources includes results such as written works (like the one in your hands, for instance), that are designed to challenge the reader to embrace and experience dramatic positive life-change, oftentimes by questioning the status quo and what they have held to be true as to a number of high-profile and impassioned issues. Alan intends for this system to impact the world for good.

Inspiration comes to Alan through reading great literary works that continually motivate him to challenge what he thinks he already knows – camping with Fran and their dogs (two at a time mind you) in their motor home in breathtaking Durango, Colorado – taking his dogs for a casual walk, where he can simply talk and commune with *the GOD within* – preparing delicious gourmet meals for Fran and their family and friends – and last, but not least, his beautiful grandchildren.

Alan and Fran live in Cornville, Arizona.

Alan can be reached by writing to him at:
P.O. Box 1197
Cornville, Arizona 86325
Or visiting his website
www.TheWalkBook.com

TITLES COMING SOON

My Weekly Walk

Angel Chance

I Am Every Woman

Made in the USA
Las Vegas, NV
25 June 2021